Eph. 3:

Peace & Hots

Brandi Volk

THE POWER
PROJECT

BRANDI VOTH

The Power Project

Quantity sales special discounts are available on quantity purchases by corporations, associations, and others. For details, contact the publisher at the address above.

Orders by U.S. trade bookstores and wholesalers. Email info@ BeyondPublishing.net

The Beyond Publishing Speakers Bureau can bring authors to your live event. For more information or to book an event contact the Beyond Publishing Speakers Bureau speak@BeyondPublishing.net

The Author can be reached directly @the-powerproject.com

Manufactured and printed in the United States of America distributed globally by BeyondPublishing.net

BEYOND
PUBLISHING

New York | Los Angeles | London | Sydney

ISBN Hardcover: 978-1-949873-54-2

DEDICATION

"This book is dedicated to all the bossy little girls that have been told you talk too much.

Stand up and own that voice Sis. You're a Leader."

CREDITS

Mattie Simmons, I wrote the book, bro.
Let's get this bread.

Mom, thanks for telling me God was going to use me special one day.

Dad, thanks for making me believe I can do anything I set my mind to.

My boys, thank you for being the coolest kids in the world who understood Mom was following her purpose in life and forgave me when I forgot to dry your laundry or sign your binder.

My husband, my soul mate, my biggest cheerleader, and the indulger of all my dreams, thanks for being such a Maverick and teaching me to take risks! You're my favorite person on the whole friggin' planet!

TABLE OF CONTENTS

FOREWORD

T he wisps of his frosty hair trembled as he shook his head back and forth, specks of spit flew from his mouth and through the air from his loud declaration. He paused to wipe an obscene amount of sweat from his brow and nape of his neck. He took a deep breath before he continued to shout, "The power of the holy spirit!" I couldn't help but become distracted with the large bulging vein in the middle of his forehead. It could not be good for his health. The louder he shouted, the redder his face became—until it was purple almost-- and the larger the vein grew. Was he going to pass out? Should someone call a doctor? My mind drifted from his stroke-like physical condition to the more confusing subject at hand. The words and the message were not lining up with the way he was delivering it. I mean, he was talking about Jesus, who not only loves us but gave His life for us. He was talking about salvation and the power that is within us. How could those subjects prompt this anger being delivered from the pulpit?

That is the earliest image of power I can recollect. He could have been one of many men. They all sounded the same to me. An old man, in a suit, standing on stage, screaming, sweating, and spitting, who was, by all definitions, the absolute authority of right and wrong. That was power. No one was to question his authority, nor should a woman admit to feeling that she was instilled with a power at work within her.

I began writing this book while on a plane to Australia as a way for me to put into words how I was struggling with my voice. It wasn't a typical struggle, however. Most people go in search of their voice or strive to strengthen and develop their voice, but not me. My mother always told me I came out talking and never quit.

You see, my struggle was different. I've struggled my entire life with having too much of a voice. I've struggled with being opinionated, headstrong. I was always speaking before I thought, and I was neither meek nor mild. But I struggled with *how* God wanted me to use that voice. I knew that he had given me a voice for a reason, I just didn't know what that reason was. What did He want me to do? How did He want me to serve?

I knew I was being led to a bigger purpose, but I didn't know how to find it. After a decade of being a stay-at-home-mom, I began running a successful skincare business that quickly expanded globally. While I experienced great success in my business and absolutely loved it, I felt a greater calling. I knew I was meant to be speaking into large groups of women, pouring into them, and empowering them. I yearned to tell other women that they, too, could embrace their voice and own their God-given power. While I was spending a great deal of time speaking to crowds of people on a regular basis, I felt as if I was being called to use my voice for something more than skincare and sales. It just took me traveling to the other side of the world to discover that exact purpose.

As you reach the end, I hope you notice an evolution throughout this book. It has been a journey of self-discovery and purpose that took me nearly three years to write. I am not the same person at the end of this book as I was in the beginning, and I am so proud of what has been created on these pages. I have learned who I truly am in Christ. I have learned to listen to God's call and lean into it. And, I have learned how to fully and whole-heartedly unlock my purpose. I would like to show you what that journey looked like for me in hopes that wherever you are, no matter what you find yourself doing in life, you too will realize that you can answer the call and own your God-given power. I've included dates throughout the book so you can see that this was not an overnight discovery. I did not just wake up one day and realize the calling on my life. It's taken time, loads of prayer to seek Him, and a significant amount of personal development. However, as I found myself typing the last sentence of the final chapter, I realized this journey I was on was actually one I had been walking my entire life. I had been following the steps of fulfilling the purpose He had for my life all along. I just had not realized each step was part of the journey. I hope that you, too, can eventually look back and see that every single step of your journey has been a stepping-stone along your path of purpose.

Will I Ever Feel Good Again?

Eyes closed. I can't quite get them open. I feel groggy. No, super groggy. Drunk? Stoned? Wait, what's that smell? It smells... sterile. And beeping, there's beeping. Everything else is completely silent except for the steady beeping. Crap! Why the hell is this bed so uncomfortable? I need to roll over. The springs of this bed are poking me in the back. Where am I? Wait. Ow. Ow. Yeah, I'm totally not going to be able to roll over. Okay, my eyes are open, and the blurry room is starting to come into focus a bit. It's dark-ish... Lights shine in from the hallway, and there is a glow of machines coming from behind me. I start looking around. Okay, things are starting to get clearer.

Wait! I had surgery. That's right. I had back surgery. Why on earth would they have such an uncomfortable bed for someone who just had back surgery? I try to say something to see if anyone else is in the room, but I can't form the words. Am I too weak? Am I dreaming? What is going on here? I look down at my hands, trying to find some way to call someone. I spot something that has a button on it. Hmm... that's either going to give me more of whatever is making me so dang confused or it might page someone. Either way, I think it's a safe bet. There's just one problem. I can't get my hand over to it. Oh, and it must be for calling the nurse because there's some other button thing taped to my finger. I'm assuming that button is the cause of whatever is making me feel like I just attended Woodstock. I can't move. I can't speak. I've barely gotten my eyes open. Crap! Dr. O'Brien lied. This was a harder surgery than he had said it was. I'm paralyzed. Great! This is going to be awesome! How am I going to ski? Or surf? Or swim? Or…

Wait… I just moved my big toe. Okay, there's one big toe. There are all the other toes on the right foot. Now for the left. Yup, okay. Good. Toes are moving. That means the legs should be good to go, too. That seems like far greater of a task than I can summon the strength for at this point. Oh my gosh! This freaking bed! I've got to get rolled over. I can't believe the springs in this thing! Okay, back to that button thing… If I can just get my hand over to it. Wait, almost there. So close. YES! Got it! I can't believe how much energy that took. Okay, it's pushed. Someone's coming in any minute to help me out with this bed. *Beep. Beep. Beep. Beep.* Well, the heart sounds normal, so they must not have screwed that up. *Beep. Beep. Beep.* Where is that nurse? I'll just push that button again… Or maybe not. Where the heck did it go? Why is it so much work to just try to turn my head? Screw it. I'll just wait. With a freshly sore post-surgery back resting on a bed with springs sticking out of it. *Beep. Beep. Beep.*

"Hi, honey. I'm Mark. What do you need?" Mark! Okay, good. Mark is here. This bed is awful, and I need you to fix it! Now! "Honey, did you need something?" Oh yeah. This talking thing. It's going to take some effort. Mark seems to have purple waves rolling across his face. And there's some blue blurry halo type of thing hovering over his head. I'm sure he's a dandy guy, but he looks pretty trippy right now. Okay, Focus. Back to the bed. Form words. Come on.

"Ish dis beddddddd. Um ro' over. Suuucks."

"I'm sorry, honey. Just a minute. Jay, can you come in here and help me, please. I'm not sure what the problem is." Jay. He looks like a lovely guy, even if he's green. Why is he green? What is wrong with his face? Oh, and he's floating all over the place. Stand still Jay. This bed sucks, and I need you to fix the dang springs. You're my only hope. Mark has no idea what he's doing. Focus. Speak clearly enough to get the bed changed out. Deep breath. Jay seems to know. He comes in and leans in closely. "Is it your back? Are you uncomfortable?" Yes. He knows. Deep breath. Clear thoughts.

"Yes! Yes! Uncomfortable! This bed sucks! Why don't you have better beds? Lean me up, please!" There. Finally. I got it out! Now they know I need a new bed.

"Honey, it's not the bed. You had back surgery. You have two rods, 26 screws, and 12 fused discs holding your spine straight. It was a big deal. You're going to be uncomfortable." Jay hooks his arm under my armpit and places his other hand on my lower back. He's gesturing for Mark to do the same thing. They're leaning me up. Oh, that's it! That feels so much better. The pressure is off. Oh no. Wait. Dizziness. I'm gonna puke. No, I'm going to pass out. No puke. I'm definitely going to... pass out... There it is. Never mind. Put me back down. My eyes are falling shut. Jay, I see Jay, yup… still green. He looks annoyed, and his eyes are rolling as he lays me back down.

"I bet she has a Tempur-pedic at home, ya think?" Mark snidely remarks to Jay as the two stifle their giggles.

What? How does he know I have a Tempur-pedic? That's exactly what I've been thinking! They're laughing. Why are they laughing? They should have Tempur-pedics for people that have just had extensive back surgery. I should tell them that. Wait, I've thought that a lot tonight. Have I already told them that? Oh, I'm too tired to think. But, they could quit laughing. In case they didn't realize, I did just have back surgery… I'm tired. Eyes closing and everything getting quiet.

"Hey Mark, did you hang another bag of blood?"

WHAT? Eyes Open!

"Yeah. That's the third bag." What? What did Mark just say? Third bag... Holy crap! I see it. I see the blood. In the bag. Going through a tube and into my vein… Someone else's blood. Into *my* veins… You have got to be kidding me? Don't they know I'm a germaphobe? I don't even drink after other people more or less allow blood from unknown people into my veins. No one told me anything about this. The panic starts to set in... What if I…crap… tired…sleep… *Beep. Beep. Beep.*

This had not been an emergency surgery. It had been well planned out. Basically, I had planned on having this surgery since I was about 16 years old. I was diagnosed with Gray Rotative, or Idiopathic Scoliosis, at the age of 11 in the fifth grade. We found it during one of those routine checks the school nurse does. All the kids in my grade lined up in the hallway and were told to bend over and touch their toes as the nurse walked behind them, checking their spines. It had been nothing out of the ordinary. I bent over and touched my toes while giggling and whispering with my friend Gina. I finished the exam and went back into our classroom to continue our lessons. Just as I had finished reading page two of our handout aloud, the nurse stuck her head in the classroom and gestured for my teacher to step outside. A few minutes later, she came back in and asked that two other girls and I go with the school nurse. We followed the nurse down the hallway to the nurse's station, where she performed another test. This time, she gave me a note to give my parents saying I needed to see a doctor for a true Scoliosis exam. What came later was an appointment at Scottish Rite Hospital for children where I fully expected to be given a clean bill of health and sent on my merry way. Dr. Johnston, however, had a different course of action in store for me. I spent the next six years sleeping in a fiberglass back brace with Velcro straps that had to be tightened up so tight I swear my rib cages were overlapping.

Due to a somewhat significant case of claustrophobia, I would wake up in a sheer panic most nights, screaming and ripping the torturous device off my body, so my dad began duct-taping me into the brace. Duct. Taped. Into a fiberglass mold that shoved my body in the opposite direction it was created. It was lovely. And only mildly uncomfortable. I remember one night when I woke up with the awful feeling of my stomach churning and a gag in the back of my throat. There was no time to get my parents to remove the duct tape from the body cast I was in, so I sprinted down the hallway past my parents' and brother's rooms to the bathroom where I proceeded to retch into the toilet with the complete and utter inability to bend. After all, the brace went from the bottom of my hips all the way up past my armpits. Bending was impossible. It was delightful. One good thing about it was it always provided great conversation for sleepovers. In the beginning, I was mortified that my parents would make me take this heinous device to friends' houses, and, in turn, I politely declined sleepovers. This really helped me make new friends at the country school I transferred to for sixth grade. I eventually got over it and decided I would just have all of my friends autograph the brace when I went to sleepovers, like kids do with casted arms. This was a real blast throughout *all* of junior high and high school!

At 18, my doctors told me the brace had served its purpose and prevented my curvature and rotation from getting any worse, so it was up to me whether or not I had to have surgery. Considering the fact I was headed into my freshman year of college, I opted out and didn't see a doctor about my spine for the next 15 years. After having my youngest child, I began having increased problems with my back. I had always been crooked, with one arm longer than the other, one leg shorter than the other, one rib cage protruding out the front of my torso, and a big hump sticking out of the right side of my back. But, it became more noticeable. My entire life, I was highly aware of my posture and how to hold my body to keep the deformity from being noticed, but it began to affect how my clothing fit. I was constantly tugging on my bra, trying to get it to stay in place. And, while my back had hurt and spasmed for as long as I could remember, I began experiencing other symptoms. My legs started aching on a regular basis, and my left arm would ache and tingle, as well as become weak and lose strength. I was terrified it might be something related to a muscular or autoimmune deficiency I had inherited from my mother, so I had all the tests done. However, no one could explain why it was happening. I could only guess it must be connected with my twisted and gnarled spinal column. My husband and I decided I would have back surgery when our youngest child went to kindergarten. We knew it would be an extended recovery with limited abilities, so we thought it would be best if both kids were gone for eight hours a day and old enough to understand why Mommy couldn't pick them up. We researched doctors for about two years because we wanted to ensure that only the best would disassemble and reassemble my spine. After interviewing multiple doctors, we decided to use Dr. Michael O'Brian with the Baylor Scoliosis Center. I mentioned to him I understood how huge this surgery was and what a major undertaking it would be, but I was incredibly nervous. He shrugged his shoulders and replied, "Not really. If you ask me to deactivate a nuclear bomb, I would have no idea what to do. But, for the guy who is trained and does it every day, it's no big deal. I disassemble and reassemble spines every day as if they're Legos. It's not really a big deal." He was cocky! And I liked it. I didn't want any of the other doctors who had hesitantly talked about the procedure. I certainly didn't want the doctor who told me he wouldn't touch my spine with a ten-foot pole. I wanted the cocky surgeon. The one who looked at spines like they were Legos. He was my guy.

The morning after my surgery, the physical therapist came in and told me that she wanted to get me up out of bed and into a chair. I knew it was crucial for optimal recovery, so I gladly agreed. I was feeling much less woozy by then. She warned me I might feel dizzy, throw up, or pass out, but that was all normal for patients the first time they get out of bed. I breathed through the pain and dizziness while telling the therapist I was okay because I was a yogi. I made it to the chair and visited with my parents. My husband and children showed up to tell me all about the trampoline park that they had been to that morning. My little one had been a little freaked out the night before when they popped in to say hi after the surgery, so it was good for them to see me awake and talking. Neither of them had ever seen mom out of commission as I had hardly even been sick with a cold before this. So, one can only imagine how scary it was for an eight-year-old to see their mom with a heart monitor, catheter, and bag of blood hanging beside her. I was able to tell them I had gotten up, sat in the chair, and was doing fine, so they were able to leave feeling much more relieved with the situation. By day four, I was moved out of ICU and to the sixth floor for recovery. I was finally able to take a full shower, and walk back and forth to the bathroom, as well as walk around the nurse's station and through the hallways. I felt great and strong. I've always recovered and bounced back quickly. I've always had a determination that allowed me to push through pain, and nothing had ever kept me down. The morning after having my first c-section, I showered myself and walked around the entire hospital, telling everyone how great I felt. Mindset is 90% of a person's recovery. Leading up to the procedure, I was convinced I could mindset myself out of anything. Various family members visited throughout the next four days, and my husband stayed by my side the entire time. I was pleasantly surprised by how well the recovery had gone. And as often is the case in life, just when we feel a little overconfident, we're brought back to reality. On the seventh and final night I was in the hospital, something changed. My muscles started viciously spasming. It felt like someone was stabbing me with an ice pick in multiple locations all over my back. I had experienced spasms before, but nothing like these. I called for the nurse, Preshti, and told her what was going on. She helped me up, and we did the stretches I had been taught to do to help combat the spasms. They didn't help. She suggested we take a walk, which is what my occupational therapist had told me would help. So, my husband, Preshti, and I took a walk. The spasms intensified as if the ice pick was being twisted inside of my muscles. We went back to my room, where she gave me more medication. I laid back down and tried to rest while all the muscles in my back twisted in the same manner as one would ring out a dishrag. I can only compare it to what contractions in the midst of labor feel like. This continued throughout the night. Preshti came back in to check on me and found me lying there with tears streaming down my face while my muscles convulsed. I told her to please give me something to knock me out. If the muscle relaxers were not going to stop the spasm cycle, at least knock me out where I could sleep. I didn't care when I woke up. I just needed rest and to be able to ignore the pain. She told me I was at the maximum level of medication she could give me. I squeezed my eyes shut as tears poured down the sides of my cheeks, soaking my pillow. I begged her to please do something. I was in so much pain and so very tired. She took a deep breath, nodded, and walked out of the room. She reappeared a few minutes later with a small white paper cup in her hand. She leaned down near my face and brushed my tear-soaked hair back from my forehead. In her soothing, calm voice, she spoke words that I will never forget.

"I can give you this medicine," she said while showing me the two white pills in the cup. "However, you may not wake up. So, I need you to tell me it's okay to give it to you." I looked into her eyes, which radiated the most warmth and love that I could have ever asked for at that moment. I looked over at my sleeping husband and realized he couldn't make the decision for me. I looked back at Preshti and asked, "What? What am I supposed to do? I'm hurting so bad. I have to sleep. But, I don't want to take too much medicine. What do I do?"

She took my hand and looked deep into my eyes, "We're going to pray, you're going to take the medicine, and you're going to rest." The soothing calm of that statement caught me by surprise. It just hadn't dawned on me she would be willing to pray with me. I trusted her. I trusted God.

"You'll make sure I wake up, right?" I asked as the tears continued to pour, and I gripped her hand firmly.

She nodded. "I'm here, and so is God. We'll pray, and I'll watch you all night." I nodded. "Tell me that you want the medicine," she told me. I took a deep breath as my muscles convulsed once again.

"I want the medicine." She leaned down, cradled my head in the crook of her arm, and whispered the most calming prayer of protection across my forehead that I could have asked for. An angel herself could not have delivered a more beautiful prayer with such a peaceful presence. I took the pills and shortly thereafter drifted off to sleep. I was released the next morning without getting to thank my nightshift guardian angel.

Unfortunately, the muscle spasms continued after that night. I spent the next four months of life recovering and enduring endless spasms. Nothing helped. They sent me home with prescriptions for hydrocodone, valium, Robaxin, as well as a large dosage of Flexerill. There was a notepad on my nightstand where my husband kept the dosages written down and what time he needed to administer the medication in order to avoid anyone confusing the dosages and accidentally overdosing me. I would tell him each night to just make sure I kept breathing. I couldn't eat much because I was constantly nauseous, and I lost so much weight I didn't even break 100 lbs. Apparently, the nerve that controls your body's response to hunger or nausea is located in your neck along the T2, which happened to be where my muscles were so tightly spasmed and infringing on all the nerves around them. Thankfully, my husband had taken five weeks off to care for the kids and me after the surgery. I look back at that time and am so very grateful for his outstanding care. He's not a nurturing person by nature, but one would have never known with the way he washed and dried my hair for me, held me at night, and let me cry on his shoulder as he showered me. We celebrated Christmas at our house four days after I came home from the hospital. Luckily, I had the entire house decorated, presents wrapped, and Christmas pajamas ready for the celebration. My parents, brother, sister-in-law, and nephew all came over to celebrate with us. The only thing I remember about that Christmas was the pajamas I specifically changed into, and the fact that I made it up and down the stairs to the family room so we could celebrate in the same traditional manner we always had. I was determined that my children would not know a different Christmas just because I had undergone major surgery.

I cried every day for four months straight. I cried because I was in pain. I cried because I couldn't do what I was accustomed to doing. I cried because my husband was having to do everything for my children and me. I cried because I felt like a failure as a wife. I cried because I felt like a failure as a mom. I cried because I didn't feel good. My children, who were 8 and 5 at this point, had never seen me cry before. Seriously, never. When we went for the Spring Fling at school, my third grader's teacher told me she asked how I was every day, and my son had answered with, "Well, she didn't cry today." I would ask my husband when I would feel good again, and he would respond with, "One day, you're going to wake up and just feel good."

This became a quote he and my dad repeated to me over and over. Each time, I wanted to choke them.

I went for my two-month follow-up and explained to my doctor I was still having awful spasms. He offered me more prescriptions, but I told them the medications were not working, so I had quit taking them. This was when he recommended dry-needling and mild yoga. I had never heard of dry-needling before, but it was explained to me as taking acupuncture needles to insert directly into the spasmed muscle and then wiggling them around in order to force the muscle to release. At this point, I would have tried anything, so I eagerly signed up. I was overjoyed to find out our local physical therapy center had a licensed dry-needling therapist so I wouldn't have to make the two-hour drive twice a week. I just needed to figure out the driving thing, so I wouldn't have to burden someone with taking me each time. I hadn't quite mastered driving yet since I had a hard time holding my head up. This was an unexpected side-effect of the surgery. I can only describe the feeling as a newborn baby who has just learned to hold his head up. It's weak and wobbly, and he can only lift it for short periods of time. I have a new compassion for newborns and their wobbly little necks. Not only were my muscles in my neck weak, but they were also so angry from the surgery, they would begin to burn when they went unsupported. When my husband would take me to town, we had to plan the trip out accordingly to account for my newborn neck. If we went to eat, I had to have a booth with a back that I could lean my head back on. And, when we drove down the road, I kept an airplane neck pillow with me at all times to make the ride a little more pleasant. Most trips resulted in me in tears on the way home from exhaustion and pain.

I had my first appointment with my sweet therapist, Cheryl. She explained how the process would work and had me lie down on my stomach while she spent the next hour placing tiny needles into the center of each spasm and manipulating the muscle to release. It was nothing for the areas of my back I had lost feeling in. Within the region of the twelve discs, my entire back had lost sensation due to the surgery. Nearly five years later, I still have areas of my back that are completely numb. However, in the areas above the incision, the problematic areas of my traps and neck, I could feel every movement of the needle. It was one of the strangest experiences. While the needles didn't really hurt as they were inserted, once they contacted the spasm, I felt like I was going to pass out or vomit. Once the appointment was over, I made my way back to the car, replaced the Velcro back brace I had to wear each time I got in a vehicle, and propped myself up in the driver's seat with all of the pillows I had brought. I placed one large fluffy pillow on my left side to provide my arm a soft resting place, so I didn't have to summon the strength to hold the arm up extending on the steering wheel for the next 17 miles home. I did the same on my right side between my body and the console. Then I placed one neck pillow around the back of my neck and one around the front. This was the magic placement I had discovered held my head mostly supported for the duration of the drive. As I turned onto the highway, I realized that this was the first time in nine weeks my muscles were not writhing and twisting in anger. I breathed a deep breath and realized that all of the muscles in my back that had been sewn back together like a patchwork quilt were quiet for the first time in a long time.

"Oh Thank God!" I thought. I had finally found something that would give me relief! That evening I was so excited to share with my husband about this treatment and how much it had helped. My kids were ecstatic to see mom happy and feeling so much better! I had also been released by my doctor to finally be able to sit in my hot tub just as long as I didn't get it too hot. He warned me that there was metal in my back that would heat up internally, and that, combined with the loss of sensation, could result in a burn. I, not wanting any undue complications with my recovery, bumped the temp down a little cooler than I would have preferred, and sat in what felt like the most glorious soak of all time! As a person who had dealt with an aching back and sore muscles on a daily basis, my hot tub is my happy place! I regularly put my kids to bed, grab a glass of red wine, and head to the hot tub to soak in peace and quiet for 30 minutes while my mind unwinds from the day. So, not having been able to soak had definitely been difficult. Back problems or not, I recommend everyone stop what you are doing right now and get a hot tub. I settled into the warm bubbles as I leaned my head back, closed my eyes, and realized that as bleak as the past nine painful weeks had been, I just might make a full recovery after all.

Eve

I went for my second dry-needling appointment. I was so excited to continue the treatments and get more relief. My muscles had started tightening back up the evening before. As I entered the physical therapy center, my friend at the front desk informed me that my therapist had a family emergency and wouldn't be able to provide my treatments for the day, but they had a different therapist who would do some stretches and massages with me. I was disappointed since the first treatment had provided me such relief, but I also wouldn't mind a massage as well. Eve, an outgoing redhead with a grin from ear to ear, came out and showed me back to my room where she would work with me. She spent the next 45 minutes massaging my back and telling me all about her other job as a nanny. She was a contract therapist where she traveled and filled in at whatever hospital needed her. She really enjoyed meeting all the new people and not being stuck at just one center. She was going to be traveling soon to Disney World with the family that she nannied for and was so excited about the trip. I told her not to get her hopes up too much because it was only the most magical place on earth for kids. For parents, it was exhausting, and for some reason, resulted in everyone's children becoming the absolute worst version of themselves. But, I was sure she would have a great time. At the end of the session, she told me that she was going to put some heat in my back. I quickly stopped her. My nurses, physical therapists, occupational therapists, hospital specialist, and doctors at the hospital had all warned very adamantly against the use of any heat on my back. Since I didn't have feeling in my back, the skin was sensitive from having been stretched and manipulated, and there was metal inside, so it was a recipe for disaster. She informed me that it would be okay. She had a master's in physical therapy for goodness sakes. She knew what she was doing. She would not put any heat on me that would be too hot. She went over to what looked like a beer cooler from a bar that I had worked at and slid the top open. Using a pair of tongs, she pulled out a white steaming towel and some sort of bladder looking compress. She laid both the compress and towel down on my table, laying her hand on top of it, and informed me that she wouldn't be able to touch it if it was too hot, so I could relax and lie my back down on it.

The entire compress went from my shoulders down to my lower back and top of my hips. I couldn't lie; the warm steam felt incredible on my angry muscles. I wished I would have done this much earlier. The doctors just had me so freaked out about getting burnt that I was really nervous about it. I asked her again if she was sure it wasn't too hot, and she assured me it was okay. She told me she would be back in ten minutes and left me lying there to relax. I closed my eyes and breathed in a deep breath of relaxation. The steam seemed to soak deep into my muscles and release any tension held. After a few minutes, I noticed myself lifting my hips up off the table. For some reason, it felt really hot on my lower back and hips. I raised them up twice more before she entered the room. I immediately asked her to check and see if this was too hot because it felt really hot on my lower back. She placed her hand between my back and the compress and assured me it was fine. It would burn her hand if it was too hot. "Five more minutes," she told me as she left the room. After five minutes, she released me, and I made my way to the front desk to schedule my next appointment with Cheryl. After scheduling my appointment, I was directed to the financial desk to pay for the session. For some reason, the sweet lady behind the counter was having a hard time with the card reader and processing my payment. While waiting on my receipt, I noticed a foul odor. "What on earth was that smell?" I thought. I sniffed deeper, looking over my left and then right shoulders trying to see where it came from. It smelled like soured laundry, but even worse than that. It was an awful stench. I assumed those towels she used must have been sour. It was gross. As I made my way across the parking lot to my car, I breathed in the fresh air outside and thought about how grateful I was to be feeling good at that moment.

I went on to pick the kids up from school that day for the first time since surgery, and they were thrilled to see Mommy in the carpool lane. On our way home, we stopped by a local gift shop and picked up a birthday gift for one of our friends and decided to take it with us to her house for a visit. She had been sweet enough to stop by and see me a few times during my recovery, but it had all been very foggy, and I wanted to see her while I was feeling good. The boys carried her gift in for me, and we chatted with her and her fiancé for a bit, telling them all about my new treatments and how much better I was feeling. It was a good day. After our visit with our friends, we came home and enjoyed a spaghetti dinner. Although I was feeling much better, I decided I needed to lay down. I made my way to the bathroom to take a shower, feeling so full of gratitude for the day of relaxation and socialization spent with family and friends while I felt good. It was the first day in a very long time I had not shed a single tear. As I prepared to take a shower, I pulled my sports bra off while I recapped the day's events in my head. I smiled to myself once again, so grateful for the joyful feeling of not hurting so badly. At that moment, I felt a bead roll across my hip and down across my rear. I thought it must be something that had fallen out of my hair or shirt, so I turned around to see what had just rolled down my backside. As I turned to look over my shoulder in the mirror, I saw not only something out of a horror movie, but I saw something that would set my recovery back an additional four months.

I walked into the living room wrapped in a towel, hair in a messy bun on top of my head and holding my breath. The tears in my eyes waited to stream down my face. The lump in my throat wouldn't let me form words. I stared across the living room at my husband in his recliner while the tears built up. He looked up immediately and asked what was wrong. I took a deep breath. "I'm trying so hard to stay positive right now!" I cried as I lost the battle to the lump in my throat and could no longer keep the tears at bay. I turned and pulled my towel down to reveal to him my back, bright red from the tops of my shoulder to the tops of my hips. There were over a dozen large fluid-filled blisters covering my back, some of which were 2-three" in diameter. One blister had already popped when I had removed my sports bra and dripped down onto my hips. This was the "bead" I had felt roll down my otherwise numb back. My husband's demeanor immediately changed from concern for me to complete and utter rage.

"What in the hell happened?!" He demanded. I sat there. I couldn't answer. I didn't know what to do. I couldn't wrap my mind around figuring out another course of action right now. And so, I sat, in the towel, in my chair and cried while he examined my back and tried to decide how to proceed. I listened to his rants and raves and desires to physically harm someone over this while I sat there questioning why on earth this would happen to me. Why, after all that I had been through, would God have let this happen to me? Why had the therapist not listened to my warnings about the heat? Why had I not trusted my own gut instincts? Why this, after the one good day that I had finally felt good?

The next four months resulted in wound care appointments twice a week to treat the third-degree burns that covered my back. I didn't have the strength to go into the physical therapy center and speak with anyone about the incident. I'm not sure if I didn't trust myself to not completely lose it on them or if I just couldn't emotionally handle the pain of seeing the person responsible for allowing this to happen to me. I had initially gone to see my nurse practitioner friend that sent me for wound care, and she took it upon herself to call the hospital and send pictures over. The hospital apologized and offered assistance for whatever I needed. I had all four months of my medical expenses billed to the hospital, and they never questioned it. As word got out about the incident, everyone asked if I had sued or was going to sue. It was the first question out of everyone's mouths. Even my husband, who was typically completely against the idea, thought we should. I admit, I thought about it. In great depths. Here I was, for the first time in my life with a pretty back, and this idiot had screwed it up in a matter of 15 minutes. My spasms were back in full force, and no one could do anything about it because I wasn't allowed heat, massage, or dry needling with the open wounds. Plus, now we could add the fact that I had a 12x12" bandage that stayed on my back constantly and had to be changed twice a week. And it smelled, horribly.

I was totally winning as a wife. My husband not only had to take care of the kids and me, and change my bandage for me, but he also had the privilege of sleeping next to someone who reeked. One can only imagine how that cut down on the whole spooning thing. If I had suspicions of being depressed before the burn, they were completely confirmed after the burn. I hurt. I smelled. I wasn't able to do what I wanted. I couldn't contribute in the least to our family. And, I wasn't sure I would ever feel good again. There was no need for anyone to ask me how I was feeling because not only did they not want to hear the answer, I didn't want to share it with them. At my four month appointment, my surgeon saw for the first time what my burns looked like in person. So far, he had only seen the pictures I had sent his office. He was infuriated. After doing meticulous work and leaving nothing but a pencil-thin line down the center of my spine, someone else came along and ruined his masterpiece. He informed me I needed to see a plastic surgeon, and he would refer me to because he feared I needed skin grafts. That was the point when I began considering a lawsuit.

When people would ask if I had sued or if the therapist had gotten fired, I would just tell them that I hadn't because she was just a young girl that screwed up. She was human and had made a mistake. It wasn't that different from the time that I, as a waitress, spilled an entire tray of ice waters on the head of a sweet 80-year-old woman. I sat there in sheer horror, watching water drip off her bluish-grey hair and onto her glasses as she rang out her blazer and assured me it was okay in between gasps. She had extended grace. She shouldn't have. I hadn't been new. I had done this for a long time and by no means should have spilled three full glasses of ice water on her head. The only difference was that she didn't need medical treatment moving forward. But, she could have. The glass could have fallen off the tray, landing on her head, and resulting in a concussion or laceration. She could have (and I was certain she was going to) had a heart attack from the shock and stress. I had made a mistake. So had Eve. However, now we were talking about another pending surgery, and I just couldn't deal with the thought of that. I gathered up all the photos from the past few months and collected notes from doctors and therapists who had assessed the situation for me and prepared to sue the hospital even though we had friends and family on staff and the board. We knew it would be a messy situation, but we needed some sort of restitution, especially if there was another surgery in my future.

At the plastic surgeon's office, I questioned him intently. Would my chance of skin cancer increase due to the burns? He assured me that it would not; however, I would have to keep the burn completely protected and hidden from the sun for a minimum of 12 months. Well, that was great, considering we lived on a lake. I asked him if I would need grafts or if this would heal okay. He explained to me that the color of the scars would fade, but the sheen of the skin would always be different. I could live with that. I had spent 33 years looking like The Hunchback of Notre Dame. I could deal with discolored skin. I went home to report to my husband that we would not need to have another surgery. He questioned whether I was going to sue. I thought for a moment... and took a deep breath. What good would it do? It wouldn't reverse the fact that I would live forever with scars. It wouldn't change the fact my recovery had been extended. It wouldn't give me back the time spent in four months of wound care appointments. What would it do? What would we accomplish with a lawsuit? It would ruin a young girl's life and career. It would bring negative attention to an otherwise efficient physical therapy center. It would cause hard feelings with family and friends that are involved with the hospital and center. But, most importantly, it would bring months of negativity and stress into my life. I firmly believe that the energy that we put out into this world is what we get back. Whether justified or not, I just could not bring that amount of negativity into my life at that time. Truth be told, I knew that I was on the verge of not being able to crawl out of the depressed state I was in. I was on the precipice of sinking and not being able to climb back out. I was afraid that the gossip, rumors, and damaged friendships of a lawsuit would sink me deeper into the hole where I might never see the light again. I could imagine the quicksand of depression swallowing me whole. I had an option, I could invite the negativity in, or I could extend undeserved grace and pray for God to help me forgive. She didn't ask me to forgive her. Actually, I haven't spoken to or seen her since the day she assured me the compress wasn't hot enough to burn my skin. But, for my own peace of mind, I needed to extend grace for my own healing. I chose to forgive and extend undeserved grace. I chose to heal and move on in peace.

And so today, as I wear a backless dress and show my scars, I think of Eve, and I'm reminded that grace is far better for the soul than vindication. I also realized that in the same manner, each day, we sinners in need of a savior are extended an even greater, more undeserved grace. We are human. We make mistakes. Daily. And yet, He forgives us and keeps loving us. Daily. And that is exactly how God used Eve to teach me about grace.

You may be facing the hardest thing you've ever gone through in your life. You may not see hope. You may be questioning God and everything around you. Know this. You can do this. You can overcome this. It may take you forgiving someone and extending grace for you to heal. But, one thing I can tell you for sure is that it will come down to your mindset.

5 Steps for Developing an Overcomer's Mindset

1. You must develop the grit, determination, and belief that you can do this; belief you can forgive, belief you can extend grace, and belief you can move past this hard thing.

2. You must realize you (according to the power at work within you) are stronger than whatever obstacle you are currently facing.

3. You will have to focus on the positive. You literally must say goodbye to any and all negativity. The negativity you allow into your mind will completely sabotage your journey

4. You will have to lean on God. This is where surrender comes in. This is when you say, "God, I can't get through this without you.

5. You will have to put in the work. You can develop the mindset, surrender your will, and only welcome positive thoughts, but if you don't take the action to actually do the work, you will not move past this obstacle, and you will not heal.

This may seem like a large task at hand, but remember, you can do hard things. And, whether you realize it right now, this hard thing is strengthening you for the journey of purpose God has laid out for your life.

CHAPTER 3

When the Dust Settles...

There's this funny thing we humans do. At least I do it anyway. Maybe you don't. While I'm going through something difficult, I have the tendency to think, if I can just get through this, it's going to be smooth sailing. This may be a necessary thought for survival. If I can just get through the nine months of pregnancy, it will be easier. If I can just make it through the eight hours of labor, it will be worth it. If I can just get through the first six months of the baby not sleeping. If I can just get through potty training. If I can just make it through the teen years. I don't know why I don't realize that every stage of life is going to have a new challenge. Life just isn't a sea of glass for us to float on. There will always be trials. Some will be greater than others. There will be seasons of rest as well. But, one thing is sure. Seasons will change, and you will have to learn to be flexible. And, sometimes, when the dust settles, you're left with a giant pile of crap to sort out.

Leading up to my back surgery, my husband and I had very clear roles. I took care of everything inside the house and the children. He took care of everything outside of the house and the money. At the time, we had two guest houses I rented out, and we used the extra cash for my personal spending money and to buy my husband gifts without it coming out of our joint account. He made all of the rest of the money that supported us. And, he worked his tail off to make sure we were well taken care of. We had lived a lovely life with great vacations, lots of toys, and whatever nice handbag I wanted.

Aside from 2009, we hadn't had to worry much about finances. That was the year when both the housing and oil market tanked at the end of 2008, and the oil market continued to plummet in 2009. In August 2008, we signed papers on our first home, the first mortgage my name had ever been on. We were moving to a gorgeous home with a shop and guest cabin on 28 acres at the lake. It was our dream home. Our other home hadn't sold yet, but that was okay. We decided we would just keep it and use it as a guest house or rental until our oldest child (my stepson) was old enough to take it over. I was 20 weeks pregnant with our second child together, and this house was going to be great for our growing family. The day we signed papers on our house, the price of oil was $130 per barrel. Since our primary income was oil production, our finances were in the black.

My youngest was born on February 9, 2009. Oil was $30 per barrel. Employees and overhead expenses still had to be paid each month, whether we got a paycheck or not. Other people's families depended on us. We knew the market was unstable. It was basically like playing blackjack every day, and trust me when I say I am Safe Bet Sally, unlike my Maverick of a husband. We always operate with a savings account that we can live on in the event that the market crashes. So, with a new baby, new mortgage, and two properties to maintain, we went into a shoestring budget mode. We cut all data plans from the house and phones, eliminated eating out, took no vacations, and dwindled our savings. Within a year, oil rebounded, and we began the rebuilding process. Over the next six years, anytime we faced a difficulty, we would remind each other we had made it through 2009, so we could make it through anything.

While going for one of my follow up doctor's appointments shortly after my surgery, we had decided to have lunch at one of our favorite spots. While we were eating, he mentioned we had spent entirely too much money on Christmas, and the credit card bill was very high. Of course, I didn't know. Very rarely did I know how much that bill was unless I had to get online and make the payment last minute. I had turned all bill paying over to him about a year before, which was a good thing considering I was out of commission for so many months. We charged everything on the credit card each month without worrying about the balance. We just paid the bill when it was due, and it was always a really big bill after Christmas. I thought it was weird that he was mentioning it, and his edgy attitude caught me off guard. We're not a couple who fights about money; we never have been. He's never been controlling, and I'm not a frivolous spender. In all honesty, I'm the one who nags about money, hence the reason the conversation caught me off guard. Since I'm the one who does all the Christmas shopping, it felt like he was directly blaming me for running the bill up so high. Besides, my neck was killing me. I had been up and about too long that day. I couldn't eat the soup and salad I would have otherwise loved because of the constant nausea and my back spasms. It was the first time I had been out of the house since the surgery, and I had been really looking forward to a day date. Now, instead, I was sitting in one of my favorite restaurants feeling terrible and fighting about money.

Not long after, while resting in the recliner, as I had every day for months, I heard the news mention oil was still on the decline with no end in sight. Apparently, it had been declining steadily for months. I vaguely remembered my husband mentioning before my surgery that the price had dropped, but I didn't realize how much it had dropped. I wasn't overly concerned. After all, we had made it through 2009, so we could make it through anything. Shortly thereafter, my husband came home to tell me we needed to put more money into the other business we had started two years prior. We started it to diversify our funds, so when oil dropped again, we would have an additional stream of income. It had been a no brainer decision. He had done the exact same thing before he was ever in oil production and turned into a very successful business. However, we hadn't taken one thing into account… losing money for two years straight. Due to some bad decisions on our part, and wrongly placed people within the company, we had been funneling money into the business for two years straight without turning a profit. It had been okay because the oil business had been supporting the new business getting off its feet. That is, until the oil business couldn't continue to support it.

The months passed, and our business situation wasn't getting better. It came to a crucial point where something had to change. We had no more money. I listened to my husband in disbelief as he shared with me the financial stresses we were under. Here we were with our new business not able to stand on its own yet and our main business not paying us. We were in a place of high debt, high overhead, and no income. I couldn't believe we were back here. Except this time, we had no savings. It was tied up in a business that was bringing in practically nothing. It was sunk in a business I had fought him from starting for quite some time. When he explained to me just how much of our own money we had poured into the business on top of the initial investment we had made, I wanted to puke. Our entire savings was tied up in it. For the past four months, I had been so wrapped up in my own recovery and depression that I had been completely oblivious that we were slowly going broke. I just sat there, letting it all sink in. Wanting to help my husband, wanting to relieve his financial burden, wanting to take his stress away, trying to decide what I had could do to help him.

And then it hit me. The resentment. I would have never told him. In all honesty, I'm not sure I have ever shared this with him. Growing up, my dad had always told me to never depend on a man but instead to make my own money. I had watched my parents fight about money all my life and had always been determined to never put myself in that position. And now, here we were. I had let someone else make the money for the past ten years without worrying about it until it was too late. If I would have pursued my own career interests, we might have had more financial stability. Since hindsight is twenty-twenty, I decided to just dig my heels in and do what it took. We knew what needed to be done, but it was going to take me helping out.

I am the very definition of a Ride or Die. If I'm in it with you, I'm with you, regardless of the circumstances. But, I will not go down without a fight. I don't quit, and I won't let you quit. I'll dig in and figure out what has to be done to fix it, and that's exactly what we did. It wasn't easy, and it took a great deal of learning on my part, but I'm happy to say the business turned around and is still going strong.

The experience changed me and us. I vowed to always have an active role in our finances and never leave my financial security dependent upon someone else. Looking back, I think this was the catalyst I actually needed to pull me out of my dismal state of pain and self-pity. I could have stayed at home and wallowed in it. I could have been still in pain, recovering from severe burns, and broke. I could have just sat on it. But I knew that wasn't an option. Would my husband have been able to do this without me? Absolutely. He's an incredibly brilliant businessman. But he asked for help. It was the first time that had happened in our marriage. I knew it was more of an emotional support role, but he needed me. So, I went into an industry in which I had no prior knowledge. I hear people say all the time they could never work with their spouse, but in all honesty, the decision was a good one for our marriage. It was really the first time we felt like equal partners in our marriage. Looking back, I realize I had always felt inferior because I wasn't bringing money in. He never thought that, of course. When I had brought up different business ventures I wanted to pursue, he would almost take offense, asking if he didn't take good enough care of me. But it was my own personal dialogue that caused the negative self-talk.

When you're trying to save a business, you inevitably have to make changes that result in hard feelings. This is even trickier when you've gone into business with friends, even if you've all agreed that there will be no hard feelings if it doesn't work out. So there we stood, with a few less friends and a lot less money in the bank. It was the single most defining time in our marriage. We had gone through a year of two major surgeries, depression, business trials, financial struggles, and friendship woes, but we still had each other. We just kept saying that if the boat sunk, we were going down together. It was good for us because it was the first time we both really had to depend on each other and felt like we were truly an unshakeable team. While fighting like hell to get the business out of the red, our marriage grew stronger. We talked daily about how strong our marriage was, how if everything else was crumbling, we were good because we had each other. And then, out of nowhere, the enemy snuck in and attacked our marriage in the midst of it all. We had clung to each other like a life raft, until we couldn't anymore and turned on each other. Problems come when you lean mind because theyavily on each other, you become tired, because you're human. At some point, you will reach a place where you can't carry each other anymore. You will come to a crossroad where you will both be tired on the same day. You'll need God to carry you at that point.

It was nothing profound, huge, or major. But we reached a point where we were simply tired. We had fought for our health, fought for our friendships, fought for our business, and when it came time to fight for our marriage, we just had no fight left in us. We either had to produce a different route or give up. We had had a lengthy, emotionally draining conversation that didn't seem like it would ever be resolved. After circling for hours, we both realized this was where we stopped. Not necessarily ended, but stopped. There was no more strength to go on. Without even knowing how we got there, we were both just done. We were exhausted from fighting against the world. I'll never forget it being the calmest, most surreal conversation one could have about ending a marriage. I spoke evenly while I explained I was tired. I held nothing against him. I asked nothing of him other than to walk away in peace, put our kids first, and always speak respectfully about each other. I thanked him for having been my best friend for a decade. I told him we had had a good run, and I would miss him, but I was done. I made a few requests of him as if it were a simple open and shut business transaction, told him I loved him, and walked out the door.

I left him to his thoughts and busied myself with the kids until my dad texted saying they were cooking at his place that night. I always feel better around my dad, so that would take my mind off things. I would just have to come up with an excuse as to where my husband was since I certainly wouldn't tell anyone what was going on. That's not in my nature. Our arguments and struggles are our own personal issues to sort out. I've learned my lesson and know that family doesn't forgive like you do. We had been at my dad's for about 20 minutes when my husband showed up. I darted my eyes across the room at him & non-verbally asked what the hell he was doing there. He just cut his eyes away and sort of shrugged his shoulders. He and my dad are close friends, which I am so very thankful for. I know the importance of your family's support in marriage. But still, this was not the time. We played nice and spent the evening avoiding conversation with each other while pretending nothing was wrong. Over the course of dinner, my dad mentioned they were going to try out a new church a friend of his had told him about. I had heard a lot about this church. I knew some people who went there, and they all had nothing but good things to say about it. My brother and his family mentioned they would go as well. This seemed like as good a time as ever for me to try out a new church, so I volunteered to go as well.

I woke up the next morning, curled up on my side of the edge of the bed, with two pillows shoved between us mind because they couldn't accidentally touch me in the middle of the night. There is no quicker way for a fight to end than for him to slide over and cuddle me in the middle of the night, and I was going to make sure that didn't happen. I was tired, and we had unresolved issues. We couldn't just pretend everything was okay. I hopped in the shower and let the hot steamy water run down over my head and across my face. I wished the water could wash all the struggles away. Wash away the six months of depression I had just gone through. Wash away the ten months of financial issues. Wash away the ominous feeling of my marriage ending. Just wash it all away. I turned the shower off, grabbed my robe, and headed upstairs to wake the boys up for church. I walked into my six-year-old's room and watched him sleeping with his round cheeks, perfectly full lips, and feathery lashes. I smiled as I remembered my husband, on the day we brought him home, saying he was the prettiest sleeper ever. He still was. I walked into my eldest's room and took in his mature features. His strong chin, jawline, and striking resemblance to his daddy. There was no hint of a baby, and very little of a boy left. He was becoming a young man. What would we tell them? How could we break up their family? They both adored their dad, but I feared my youngest would never forgive me. I squared my shoulders, put a smile on my face, and cheerfully woke both boys up with hugs and giggles. I left them to get ready for church, and headed downstairs, feeling even heavier than I had before.

As I rounded the corner, I noticed the bedroom light was on, and as I walked in, my husband was getting dressed. In a rather combative manner, I asked what he was doing. "I thought I'd go to church with you, if that's okay," he replied. This was not normal for our marriage. He had gone to church with me at the last church we attended, but it had never been due to his own free will. I stood standing in the room, with what most likely looked like the least inviting face possible and replied, "Sure. But we're still getting a divorce." For the life of me, I still don't know why on earth he chose to go that day, other than God was talking to one of us, and somebody listened.

We walked into the church that morning, with a crew of oblivious family members. As far as they knew, all of us were one big happy family going to church. We were greeted by an incredibly friendly group of church volunteers, but not overly friendly in the weird way that makes you feel like they are pouncing on you because you are fresh meat ready to have your soul saved. We checked the kids into Sunday school and settled in for the sermon. The music was fantastic, and the congregation was warm.

Then our pastor began preaching over marriage. He talked about how our best bet to having a happy marriage was to stay in the one you are in. He spent the entire message preaching over staying married and how things wouldn't be easier if you quit. My husband immediately reached over, took my hand, and we both cried throughout the entire sermon. We were silent as we drove down the highway with the kids in the backseat, and then he spoke the first words we had really spoken to each other in a couple of days. "Well, that was a good message. I think we're supposed to stay married and go to church there. What did you think?" I smiled at him through tears and told him it felt like home. We went home and had a long talk where we hugged, cried, and promised to not give up on each other.

You can read all the statistics you want about the number one cause of divorce, but the truth is that people get divorced because they give up. Sure, there are circumstances where it is a toxic, unhealthy, or abusive relationship, and both parties are better off going their separate ways. However, the majority of divorces are because the couple is tired, and they give up. To be clear, God didn't save our marriage, at least not in the way Christians expect Him to fix things. He doesn't do that. He doesn't snap his fingers and make all of your problems go away. He did send words of encouragement that we both needed at a time that our hearts were open. However, we put the work in to stay married. We committed to communicating better, committing to work, and developing a stronger mindset that we would not ever give up. Has it been rainbows and butterflies ever since that morning in church? Heck no! We are human. And, we're the two most hard-headed, stubborn individuals you may ever meet. We still have hard times. We still have days that it feels like it would be easier to just give up. But we don't quit. We keep going. We keep growing. We keep working. We've developed an "us against the world" mentality. The problems come against us, not between us. And now, we have God fully intertwined in our marriage. He is the fundamental key to carrying us through the hard times, and sometimes He is the one thing holding us together. We now know that when we can't carry each other, He has us both.

Marriage is hard. You are committing to one person for the rest of your life in spite of their flaws and yours. There will be times you will give the rest of the world the best of you, and your spouse will get the crumbs. Actually, this is an all too common occurrence. The world will inevitably come between the two of you. You will want to give up. If you're not careful, you can convince yourself it would actually be easier to just throw the towel in. And, if you don't acknowledge that, you're setting yourself up for failure. You will each need to work daily at forging the strongest marriage possible with God at the center. But, I will let you in on the key secret to having a successful marriage: Just don't quit.

5 Tips for Staying Married (Even When You're Not Sure You Want to):

1. Find a group of friends who will support your marriage and pray for you.

2. Find a church you both enjoy that will pour into your marriage.

3. Never let anyone come between the two of you. This is an important and often overlooked step. If they don't encourage your marriage, they're not allowed in your life. Period. Next to God, your marriage is the most important relationship in your life.

4. Let your spouse in on the problems you struggle with and seek out a solution together. The victory will create a stronger bond.

5. Have fun together in a space where none of the problems are relevant. Be goofy, free, and laugh. Allow each other the freedom to fully embrace the fun times.

CHAPTER 4

The Meek Will Inherit the Earth

I think it's important to explain where I came from and what formed me. Far too often, we believe we wake up one morning and discover our purpose when God created us for purpose in the beginning. Every part of our journey has been implemental in creating us to be who He calls us to be. That was difficult for me growing up. I wasn't sure why he would create me in the manner He did, or how I would use that to serve Him. My entire life, I grew up looking at my grandma (NanNaw) as the epitome of a wife, mother, grandmother, and Christian woman. She's humble, modest, meek, caring, sensitive to others' needs, thoughtful. My grandmother is the epitome of that scripture: "She rises up before her family to prepare the meal." She had breakfast ready by six o'clock every morning when I was a kid, and we knew that we, along with my uncles, and all of my PawPaw's employees were welcome to come have biscuits and gravy with bacon and eggs. Her bed was made, and she would either be dressed or in a housecoat. She read her Bible daily and was a massive prayer warrior. I'm convinced she's the sole reason I made it through my late teens and early twenties.

She and my grandpa had four boys, but she desperately wanted a girl. So, you can imagine her excitement when the first grandchild came out and was a girl. I've been told "she dropped her quarter three times trying to put it in the payphone to call my grandpa and tell him, 'It's a Girl!'" To say I was rotten is an understatement. If I come across as high maintenance, I blame it solely on my grandparents who spoiled me to no end. I was fitted in the most beautiful Martha's Miniatures dresses one could imagine. The frilly, elaborate dresses equipped with smocked collars, yards of lace, and loads of tulle came from an upscale boutique in my dad & grandpa's birth town. These dresses were top of the line and were topped off by a jingle bell sewn into the underside of the smock. Not only did I "swoosh" when I walked, but I jingled as well! At Easter, the look was topped off with a hat, lace gloves, purse, white leather shoes, and frilly lace-lined socks. In order to keep my grandpa from lecturing about the amount of money spent on my wardrobe, she would bring the dresses home and hide them in the closet for a couple of weeks before I could wear it. That way, when he asked if it was a new dress I was wearing, we could both tell him I had had it for a little while. You see, in addition to her Godly traits, she was absolutely incapable of telling even a little white lie. She is, however, the Master of Creative Wording. Anyone in our family knows that if you ask her how she likes something, if she shrugs her shoulders and answers, "it's different" … she hates it!

She plays the piano beautifully. Our entire family is musical. My grandpa and father played the bass. My three uncles play the drums, guitar, and bass. They are all self-taught and play by ear. That trait was passed onto the grandchildren. They can all play instruments and have the voices of angels, except for my brother and me. That gene skipped us... My NanNaw, however, did not accept that. She had dreams of me being a great pianist. She bought me a keyboard for Christmas, and she and my grandpa paid for me to take lessons for a year. She would pick me up from school and take me to the lessons and follow up throughout the week to ensure I was practicing. However, I hated piano! I can't "hear the note" and "know what key I need to be in"… Not my jam! I wanted to take drum lessons! My cousins did, and it looked so fun to bang away on those bad boys! But I was informed that wasn't ladylike, and girls don't play the drums. She would sit at the piano with me playing "At The Cross" and have me listen for the notes and keys. She had a grand dream of me singing it at church one day and spent countless hours trying to vocal train me, because if I couldn't play the piano, I at least had to learn to sing. I'm not really sure at what point she gave up and realized music was not in the stars for me, but eventually she just went back to playing the piano and singing, while I laid on the couch and listened to her.

Her house was immaculate! Not just neat and clean, but organized to a tee, a place for everything, and everything in its place! To this day, if I need a flashlight or batteries, I can find them in the same drawer where they've always been. She always had the crispest, coldest sheets. I remember being a girl and telling her I loved her "cold" sheets. She was puzzled and asked why they would be warm if no one had been in the bed yet. I still can't quite explain the sensation, but those cold, crisp, tightly made sheets were the absolute best to slide between. She is an incredible cook! Old school southern style cooking! One mention of her chicken fried steak, chocolate pie, or biscuits and gravy and my mouth is waters immediately. She's a great pie baker and encouraged me to bake. She would pull a chair up to the counter for me to stand in, set out the ingredients, and make a dough base for me So I could then add my own ingredients to in order to come up with my own concoction. I loved that game. It was so much fun to knead the dough and mix the ingredients together with my hands. One day while doing this, I thought I would get fancy and throw out some of the ordinary ingredients in to see what I could come up with. I don't remember the exact spices I chose, but I do know that it smelled so terrible while baking, my Grandpa made us pull it out of the oven and throw it out back. The dogs didn't even deem it edible.

We had family friends we did everything with while I was growing up. Hunting at the deer camp, fishing at the lake, camping, vacationing—everything. And, it just so happens that my childhood sweetheart was in that family. I'm fairly certain that before I was even a year old, our marriage had been arranged between our families. It's funny looking back to think about how I might not have ever been interested if it wasn't expected. Who knows? What came first, the chicken or the egg? Anyway, we spent countless hours together and had a constant on again off again relationship from 2-16 years old. One weekend, in the 8th or 9th grade, we were camping at the lake, and I was over at his grandparent's camper with him watching TV. It was hot, and we were being lazy. His grandma was making vegetables for dinner, the men were frying fish outside, my grandma was in her camper, making dessert, and his mom was in hers cleaning up. NanNaw came over and asked me if I would come to the camper. I jumped up and went over, and she said, "Don't you want to help me, or one of the other ladies with something?" I looked at her a little dismayed because cooking was *not* my jam. Never had been one, never would be. On the top 20 list of things I was interested in spending my time doing, it didn't even come close to making the list. However, I *love* my NanNaw. She can ask me to do just about anything, and I will gladly say yes. So, feeling a little guilty about lazing around while the rest of them worked, I asked what she needed help with. She turned around the kitchen, pointing to the different things that were finished, and she couldn't quite come up with what I needed to do. Still confused, I asked her why she had asked me to come help if she had it all under control. Her response was, "Well, if you want him to like you, he needs to know you can cook. You don't want him thinking you're lazy. Men don't want to marry a woman that can't cook."

Okay… hold up… My response was, "One, I can't cook. Two, he and I were *both* being lazy and not helping out. Why should I hop up and pretend to be "being" busy in order for him to like me? I don't cook, and there's no sense in me pretending. He can take it or leave it. And three, when I decided to get married, if I did indeed decide that, my husband can cook and I'll make the money." She closed her eyes, which I'm convinced was a brief prayer where she asked God why on earth *this* was the girl He had blessed her with). She then rolled her eyes, shook her head, and said my name in the way I've heard her utter it throughout my life when she doesn't know what else to say. I just proceeded to go back to watching TV and sipping my drink.

My grandpa was a great man He loved God and his family. He worked hard and played hard as well. In his short 60 years, he shoved more quality of life in than most people will who live to see 100. He had a big personality and loved to argue. Quite possibly, the most stubborn man I've met, next to my husband. He lived a simple life and enjoyed it to the fullest. Coming from a line of entrepreneurs himself, he started his sandblasting and painting business in the '70s and worked his tail off to turn it into a highly successful career that employed all of his sons at one time or another and many others. I have no idea what kind of money he made, but I do know he believed in enjoying life. He loved spending money and spoiling those he loved. He valued working hard and taking care of his family. I can assure you; I never wanted for anything as a kid… except for a horse. However, he did tell my dad if he would fence the pasture, he would buy me a horse. I never got the horse, but the fence is now in place years later. As more grandkids were added to the family, my grandma was adamant (and still is) about keeping things fair across the board. What gets spent on or given to one must be to all. I went everywhere with my grandparents, even as a teenager. I was one of the few 15-year-olds who you would find on the weekends hanging out on their grandparent's lake porch, reading a book, and drinking a Dr. Pepper.

My grandpa was infamous for just packing up and heading out of town with no set plans. He would call on Friday and ask if we wanted to go eat seafood. Three hours later, we would be at the best seafood buffet with the biggest crab legs in the state of Texas. He would pick us up for dinner, and we would end up three states away because he felt like taking a road trip. We never had bags packed for these trips. His motto was we could buy anything we needed at Wal-Mart. I relished this because it meant I could literally get anything I wanted. On one such trip, I found a gold plated Marvin the Martian watch in the jewelry department I just fell in love with. For some strange reason, he was the one and only cartoon character I ever cared about. I'm still not sure what that connection was all about. I, of course, asked my PawPaw if I could get it. He obliged me as he often did, but NanNaw, in her stern lecture voice and cutting eyes, said, "Hon, you've got eight others to think of." To which he replied, "Well, if they want to get new stuff, they need to be with us. This is the one who chooses to be with us now." And, that was his philosophy in life. Be present. Live in the now. Work hard, take care of those you love, shower them with presents, and make sure your wife can stay home to take care of the house and kids. You can see where this may have been a hiccup in our otherwise undying adoration for each other.

As much as we loved each other, we loved to argue and debate. I feel like he knew I would need to be a strong enough woman to fully embrace my voice one day and not be afraid to speak up. He constantly challenged me to do just that: voice my opinion, argue my point, support it with facts, and never, ever back down from my position. One evening, when I was a junior in high school while sitting at the dinner table with both of my grandparents, the topic of college and my career plans came up. They were asking what my plans were because they knew I was very self-motivated, ambitious, and career-driven. I had big plans for myself. I explained to them that I had received a scholarship to a private liberal arts college and was going to major in International Studies. My grandpa, having never heard of this major, asked what on earth I planned to do with that since we lived in a small town, and there wasn't really a demand for that. I went on to explain I would go to law school afterward to become an International Corporate lawyer, and then go on to work for the foreign service or perhaps become an ambassador. Although, I explained, that was a position typically reserved for those born into wealth. He chewed his dinner as he mulled the concept over, and my sweet little NanNaw looked at me and asked why I was going to college anyway if I planned to get married. You can imagine her disappointment when I explained I was in no rush and not even certain I wanted to get married anyway. This was me at 18. An International Studies Major, Most Likely to Succeed, GPA of 3.99, and determined to change the world! It's funny with all the accolades, awards, grades, and test scores, I still doubted my actual God-given talents. I truly believed I was talentless.

In high school speech class, we were assigned a How To speech. Being a pro at speaking, I wasn't concerned with having to speak in front of the class like several of my classmates were. Instead, I was struggling to find a topic. I wasn't sure what knowledge I had that I could teach others. Much to my athletically inclined father's dismay, I was not an athlete and had finally accepted that fate. Much to my naturally born piano player NanNaw's disappointment, I couldn't play an instrument. Despite years of failed attempts, I could not juggle. And, well, everyone knew I had no culinary talents. So, what on earth could I teach others how to do? I decided to bring in backup and welcome my family's input. I asked my younger brother first what talents I had. "You give really good speeches." Awesome, but I couldn't give a speech about a speech. I went to my mother next, telling her that I had to give a speech about a talent that I had. "Oh, you are such a great public speaker!" She told me. We were 0 for 2 at that point. I needed a legitimate talent I could teach others to do. I called my dad up. "You're good at speaking." I was getting nowhere with these people and quickly realized I had no true talent. But I still had a secret weapon in my arsenal. I would call up NanNaw. She was my biggest fan in the whole wide world, so proud of me, and would surely be able to point out my talents the others were overlooking.

I dialed her number, and after she picked up, I said, "NanNaw, I have an assignment at school and need to teach people how to do something I'm good at. What talent do I have?"

She thought for a moment. "Talent? Let me see, Brandi. Well, you're really good at talking." And, there it was. All of the people who loved me best could come up with nothing else I was good at other than talking. The one thing they had all been telling me to do less of my entire life, and this was my talent. Great. How could you teach someone to do something that came as second nature to you as breathing? I sat down with my notebook and started writing out a speech. "How To Speak." And thus, my first speech that taught others how to give a public speech was born. I made an A+, and the teacher commended me on my topic of choice, expressing how important of a talent this was for one to possess. And yet, it would take me approximately twenty years to realize the talent that God had gifted me. God gave me a voice. I just had to use it. I find that all too often, people struggle with realizing their natural gifts. We tend to get so caught up in looking at other's talents and successes that we overlook the ones that we possess, the ones that are our unique gifts bestowed upon us. What if you quit looking around and started looking up? What if you quit seeking approval from others and started asking for his guidance. What if you quit feeling like an imposter and stood proudly in the role he had called you to? Your gift may further the kingdom, but you have to unlock that purpose first, and to do so, you have to own your power.

How to Own Your Power:

1. Get out of your own way. Quit believing you don't already possess the power needed to unlock your purpose.

2. Quit thinking your talents and gifts have to look like anyone else's.

3. Become intentional about realizing your power. Take the Strength-finder & Enneagram tests. Identify who you were created to be and how you serve the community around you.

4. Think back to when you have most felt like your truest self in life. In what moment did you most feel alive, exhilarated, and called?

5. Don't overlook or underestimate what people compliment you on. Pay attention to those gifts and develop them.

CHAPTER 5

Little Girl, Big Dreams

lose your eyes. Take a deep breath. Imagine yourself at ten years old. Who were you? Were you playing house, taking care of babies, dreaming of being a mommy one day? Perhaps you were racing the boys on the playground and dreaming of being a track star. Did you love dance and want to grow up to be a ballerina? Maybe you had a heart for animals and wanted to commit your life to taking care of them. Did you perform productions for your friends and family hoping one day you would be on stage? Doctor, lawyer, nurse, teacher, singer... What title did you hope to achieve?

Third Grade, 1991: I scooted up to the podium and took my place while an older gentleman in a navy suit adjusted the microphone for me. I moved my patent-leather dress shoes forward just a bit to gain my balance on the chair I was standing on. I calmly laid my notes down and glanced at them one last time before looking up at the room full of suit-clad businessmen-- and my mom. It was my first public speaking appearance, and I was pumped! My hair was curled and teased with an appropriately placed bow, and I had on my favorite frilly dress. I scanned the Holiday Inn conference room and took in the crowd. Adrenaline was pumping through my veins, and I couldn't wipe the smile off my face! This is what I was born to do! I opened my mouth and proceeded to share with the room full of Rotarians all about my third-grade Gifted & Talented class. After I had delivered my speech, the gentlemen all came up to me shaking my hand and thanking me for sharing. One suit-clad, white-haired gentleman came up, patted me on the back, and said, "Watch out, Ann Richards!" It certainly made my politics-loving nine-year-old self beam with pride. And, while I was thrilled this gentleman would compare me to my role model, I thought he might be a tad short-sighted. You see, I had plans to be the first female president.

You never have to tell kids to dream big. We are all innately born curious, and with the ideology that we can do anything that we want until someone tells us that we can't. I also believe none of us are born with confidence. It is developed. It just so happens no one told me I couldn't. I was raised by parents who spoke life into me, and in turn, I developed this crazy belief I could do anything I set my mind to.

I firmly believe the support system and people that you surround yourself with determine your level of confidence. I don't believe people are born insecure, just like they aren't born confident. In 2017, I went in search of how to coach confidence. In the business I'm in, I had found an alarming number of women who lacked greatly in this department. It saddened me to my very core. I desired for them to see what I saw in them: their talents, abilities, gifts, and what God had created within them. After discussing with one team member my apparent confidence and her lack of it, I asked her how she thought I could teach others to be more confident. She looked me straight in the eye and said, "You can't. We have to learn it on our own." And, she was right. I've read, researched, and studied for months, and it comes down to that simple statement. You have to learn it on your own. I credit my support system as a huge part of why I am a confident female. My mother told me all my life that Jesus was going to use me special someday, and my Dad told me I could do anything.

That isn't to say I don't have normal insecurities. Of course, I do. I'm a human. We are great at letting insecurity creep in. But, I remind myself that Satan is a liar! Don't for one second think that fear and doubt don't rear their ugly heads and creep into my psyche occasionally. But, thanks to my parent's voices in my ear, I know I can do anything I put my mind to, and God is using me for something special. Perhaps you weren't raised that way. I get it, and I find that to be an all too often occurrence.

It saddens me so much, and that is one of the reasons I am writing this book. We can change your internal dialogue. I can't give you a step by step guide to gaining confidence for you to wake up tomorrow, a fully confident woman walking in purpose. However, what I can do along the way in this journey is support you, praise you, love you, and tell you that you can do it because you are fearfully and wonderfully made. I believe the best way for people to learn what they are capable of is to witness the journey of others that have gone before them. That is how I learn the best, from watching those that have achieved what I would like to achieve myself. If you'll allow me to give you a few tangible steps that I personally implemented along the way, I promise to walk you through a beautiful illustration of discovering purpose one step at a time.

First, you have to be willing to stretch, grow, try, and inevitably fail. And then, get back up and do it again. You see, it's only through that willingness to fail that you will become more confident at trying. Every time you fail, you learn something. Through that lesson, the next attempt is less scary because you have the previous lesson in your toolbox. And, little by little, you'll gain confidence in your abilities. That is the true definition of confidence: a willingness to try and fail over and over again.

Second, you have to commit to putting the work in to become more confident. That starts with a dialogue that sounds like "I am worth investing in myself to improve my self-confidence. I can do all things through Christ who strengthens me. I can do anything I put my mind to. God is going to use me for something special one day." I like myself. I love myself. And people like me! Listen, I was the biggest eye roll skeptic at those "affirmation" speakers, too. What we tell ourselves is what we believe. The inner dialogue with yourself is second only to the voice of God in your life. This is incredibly important if you haven't been surrounded by people your whole life telling you you can do anything you set your mind to. It is up to you to become your biggest advocate.

Third, how do you feel about personal development? As a kid, my mom had a huge selection of self-help books she kept on the shelf in the bathroom. Every time I went in there, I would look through the titles and think it was so weird! I couldn't understand why anyone would want to read books that didn't entertain them. And why were they called self-help anyway? I hated the term "self-help." But, here I am now, middle-aged, and a self-proclaimed personal development junkie. I can't tell you the last book I read simply for entertainment. And, I have a wide variety of podcasts I subscribe to as well. I wish I would have been doing this type of work my entire life. I could have probably saved myself some trouble in my early twenties when I was "finding" myself.

Once I discovered all the personal development that was available for free, I became obsessed. If there was a woman speaking her truth and empowering other women, she was in my ears. If there was anyone teaching about business, I subscribed. What I didn't realize along the way was these creators would become virtual mentors of sort for me. It's worth noting I don't align or agree with everything that these hosts discuss on their shows or authors write in their books. And, that's okay. I can take the good from what they have to say, feel inspired, increase my confidence, and leave whatever it is that I disagree with behind. That is the beauty of humanity and free speech. I can assure you that someone at some point will not agree with something I have to say here, and I'm okay with that. No one is 100% right about everything, and while these people are mentors to me, they certainly are not my end all be all. As you discover new voices, take what you like, and move on. The only book on the face of the planet not up for negotiation or interpretation is the Holy Bible.

The point is, find what makes you feel confident, inspires you, or motivates you, and inundate your mind with it. What you put into your mind is what you will believe about your life. I am in a constant state of learning and becoming the best version of me that I can. My radio is only tuned to music when the kids are in the vehicle with me, or it is an unprecedented beautiful day. Otherwise, you'll find a podcast playing over the speakers.

I realized one day, as a young mother, that I had quit reading. My entire life, I had loved reading, but for some reason, had stopped.

And, coincidentally enough, this was the period of my life when I was experiencing the most in my life. Rather than filling my mind with resources that would fuel me, I was checking out Facebook during the day and trashy reality TV in the evening. Don't get me wrong; my guilty pleasure still is watching overly-privileged women make fools out of themselves on television. For the life of me, I do not know why, but I am highly entertained by them. At this point, I found myself restless and questioning whether I was created to fully and solely serve as mother to my children, or if there was something else for me. When I stopped to think about it, I realized that I couldn't even remember the last book I had read other than a children's book. I had quit reading, and in such, quit learning and growing as well. The only way to bring to life a way of life that you don't see in your close proximity is for someone to tell you about it. That is the beauty of books. There is an entire world of possibility out there written on the pages of books and, thanks to modern technology, told through the speakers of iPhones. All too often, I hear women tell me they don't have time to read. That is an excuse, and we all know what excuses are like. "Not having time" is not and will not ever be a valid excuse for anything. We have time for what we make time for. And now, with the development of modern technology, there is literally no excuse. That lie that you continue to tell yourself may very well be the one obstacle standing in the way of you achieving your dreams. Just because you're "not a reader" does not mean that you cannot become a reader.

Fourth, surround yourself with like-minded people. What does that mean? Does it mean you believe exactly the same way? Does it mean that you only allow "yes people" around you? Does it mean that you will wholeheartedly believe every word that comes out of the mouths of your peers? No. It just means you should surround yourself with people who not only believe they can do it, but that you can as well. People who refuse to let you settle, people who will push you to be the very best version of yourself and never allow you to make excuses. Fill your tank up with these people. These are your people! Spend as much time with them as you can and share with each other your goals and dreams. Support their dreams, and let them support yours. If they for one second tell you that you can't do something, they are not your people. Love them, but don't listen to them. If there was never more truth than in this quote, it's now. "Never take advice from someone you would not trade places with," which is a random quote I live by. The immediate space surrounding you should be filled with individuals who are positive people with grateful hearts.

Over my lifetime, when I look at the ones who have lifted me up the most, they are not Gossipy Gails or Negative Nancys. They are the ones who can see beauty and hope in life. They are the ones who believe in themselves, the greater good, and our combined strengths. They are the ones who will tell you to put your big girl panties on when you don't feel like getting dressed. These people are the ones who will speak life into when you feel like you have no fight left in you. If your girlfriends only sit around talking about others in a negative manner, there is no confidence building taking place. That is the absolute opposite of empowerment, and we do not build a stronger foundation by tearing others down. If they will talk about those people in front of you, they will talk about you in front of those people. While we are busy tearing each other down, we leave the door wide open for men to step in and achieve the goals we should be chasing. I don't know how we women as a whole arrived here. I don't know why sitting around in a group talking smack about others can somehow be so strangely satisfying. I check my heart daily and strive to only speak about others in an uplifting manner. It can be tempting, but when I feel myself getting sucked into that black hole, I literally remove myself from the situation both physically and mentally. I've found that to be the easiest way to not get involved.

I want you to know that if I can do it, so can you. Part of my success in life has come from this brazen belief within me that says we are all human, and no one is any more special than me. No one is off-limits. No one is untouchable. I can reach out to anyone I choose and gain wisdom from their insight. That is exactly why I am here. I want you to know I am not off-limits, and you can reach out to me. No one is more qualified or more called than anyone else. Some just have the support system in place to boldly step out in confidence and answer the call. Hopefully, you are already feeling more confident.

I sat next to a young lady on the plane one day who complimented me on my confidence. She asked how I had been able to achieve such confidence, and it was the first time anyone had so clearly asked that question. While it was true I had always been a confident female and had been surrounded by a support system that built me up, I, too, had to admit I felt more confident at that point in my life than I ever had before. I thought to myself and then smiled before answering her, "I have always been a confident person with a great support system. However, it wasn't until I truly understood who God created me to be and began fully walking in the purpose that He called me to that I became the confident woman you see in front of you. Now, I know that He made me this way for a reason. And, I know that He called me to be this person to fulfill the role that He created only me for. So, yeah. I'm pretty stinking confident in who I am today."

How to Become More Confident:

1. Be willing to fail.

2. Commit to putting the work in.

3. Dig into personal development.

4. Surround yourself with likeminded people.

CHAPTER 6

My Charmed Life

I had a good, mountain-moving friend say to me one day that those of us who are successful in business and fighting the good fight for the greater cause are those of us who have been through hard stuff. We have grit because, at one point or another in our lives, it's been necessary for our survival. I saw this statement through my then-lens of complacency and thought she must have been mistaken. I had never really been through anything that hard. My life had been pretty sweet. I had lived a charmed life.

I thought about her words while sitting through an advocacy training class. I had never known abuse. I had been protected, encouraged, and loved. I had had a beautiful childhood. Why on earth would God call me to advocate for those that had not had such favor in their lives? I didn't know how to empathize with them. I couldn't understand the trauma they went through. I had no way of wrapping my head around their decisions. That was my internal dialogue while I sat listening to other advocates speak about being called to this fight because of the childhood trauma they had endured, the addiction they had overcome, or the abusive relationship they narrowly escaped. I had had a good life. How would this purpose apply to my personal connection? In all honesty, I wanted nothing to do with the seedy and dark mission in the first place.

I grew up in a 1600-square-foot ranch-style, brick home on two acres. My very best friend in the whole world lived across from me. Summers were long, and we ran wild and free. We had a half-mile of blacktop roads to ride bicycles down that had the perfectly graded slope to coast downhill without peddling while our hair flew free in the wind that warmed our shoulders as we sped through it. My backyard backed up to a fenced-in pasture with grazing cows, but just on the other side of that pasture was where adventure awaited. We spent countless hours hiking and exploring that land.

My family lived modestly, and my dad was self-employed. I never remember wanting for anything. Don't get me wrong, money was always important to my family. We were always on a budget, and I knew when eating out was not in the budget. We were always dressed nice, but our clothes were typically K-Mart finds, unless NanNaw took us shopping. That's when we got the nicer stuff. We had a camper, a boat, and four-wheelers. We had a pretty average American life where we learned the value of working and playing hard. Some of our family's favorite memories revolved around camping on the hunting camp. The camp was more about quality family time than it was about actual hunting. We, along with my grandparents, cousins, aunts, and uncles would camp in campers out in the country on a spot of landed covered with scrub brushes and mesquite trees and inhabited with rabbits, squirrels, coyotes, foxes, bobcats, roadrunners, turkey, rattlesnakes, and whitetail deer. The nights spent around the camper under the midnight skies and twinkling stars gave us some of the best laughter and family stories. I can envision my grandpa grilling steaks over the open fire, scenting the air with the smell of slightly charred meat. I had a younger cousin who was the most hardheaded stubborn kid, and we all enjoyed giving him a hard time. One such evening, while gathered around the campfire, my brother was teasing him while telling him the sky was green. Our cousin adamantly argued back that the sky was blue. His younger brother, the sweetest, most sincere kid you would ever find, looked up at the night sky with his big eyes and very plainly stated in his little kid voice, "Wight now, it's bwack."

I grew up Pentecostal, through both sides of my family. My mother was sick my entire life. She was diagnosed with an autoimmune disease when I was about four years old. The religious leaders in our lives preached if you allow God to heal you and have faith in Him, then doctors and modern medicine need not apply. If you didn't receive the healing you asked for, you simply did not have enough faith. So, we were not vaccinated. This resulted in a summer spent quarantined in our house. The doctors didn't even want us to come into the office because we were so contagious. I was three at the time.

My mother put a tent in her bedroom with the vaporizer and breathing machine inside of it as well as our toys. She would create stories and tell us that we were playing house in order to convince two toddlers to stay put long enough for us to inhale the medication. At the time, we lived in an older rent house with a ceramic tub, and I remember one night watching my baby brother in the bathtub start coughing uncontrollably and turn blue in the face. Both of my parents hurriedly rushed me out of the bathroom while they tried to get his respiratory distress under control. Eventually, he started breathing well enough, but he was left with a cough that resembled a walrus begging for a fish. I don't remember ever feeling scared during those months. Still, at some point, I must have realized the possibility we might not recover from the illness because after we rebounded, I would testify during "testimony service" at church every single week and thank Jesus for healing me from the Whooping Cough. Literally, every single week, until my mother informed me that Jesus got the point. In all honesty, I think that I just wanted to have a testimony so badly, and that was all I had to use.

Being raised by a physically ill and weak mother is quite possibly the single most determining factor of my life. I had to be self-sufficient from an early age. My dad was and is an amazing man. But he was and is a workaholic. Nurturing was not his forte. He's a "you're tough, you can take it" kind of guy. I attribute my can-do attitude to his hard-ass ways. This was also a major deciding factor of who I am today.

I was tough because I had to be tough. I had to be tough for my mom who couldn't be for herself. I had to be tough for my younger brother, who needed a protector. I had to be tough for my dad because he told me to. And, quite frankly, thank God he did. I didn't always see it that way, however. I recall one time at a young age; I was crying over getting hurt doing something. He wiped my tears from my face and said, "You're tough. Take it like a man." I had heard this phrase all my life. Typically, I would wipe the tears away, suck it up, and square my shoulders. This was not that day. I just felt an overwhelming sense of anger and resentment. Was he stupid? Was his head actually that thick? I looked up at him through the tears, and with all the strength I could muster, shoulders squared, and voice assertive, screeched to him, "But I'm not a man! I'm a little girl!" His face softened as he chuckled, drew me closer to him, squeezed my shoulders, kissed me on the forehead, and released me. That was it. All the validation I needed. I didn't need him to coddle me or make a big production out of it; just acknowledge me, be a soft spot to land, and release me. I owe so much of my strength, grit, and tenacity to him. He believed in me. He knew I was tough. He knew I was destined for greatness. He knew I would exist in spaces where men dominated, and he taught me I damn sure better be able to be tough and take it like a man.

Despite the charm of my childhood, with cherished family memories, grandparents who spoiled me rotten, and parents who spoke strength into me, I also lived in a house with a great deal of fighting. They were just trying their best to navigate marriage, parenthood, and a chronic illness. Plus, just like in any marriage, they were two flawed humans with very different upbringings, which inevitably led to arguments. For as long as I could remember, my parents found something to fight about. It was so constant I took it upon myself to guard my brother from it. When they fought, I would take my brother to his room and distract him with something so that he didn't hear them yelling at each other. No one asked me to do this, but at an early age, I deemed myself his protector. We didn't face any actual harm in our family, and he didn't need protecting from our great life, but I felt he needed to be sheltered from the emotional toll of the arguments. It was for this very reason, when our parents split up while we were in high school, his world was completely rocked. It's amazing how two people growing up in the exact same house can have two completely different perspectives. I had expected my parents to divorce for the majority of my childhood, but it completely took him by surprise. They did, true to their co-dependent pattern, give it one more shot after I was out of high school, and then finally, when I was an adult starting my own family, gave up the battle. It's interesting how you can see the crash coming for years and brace for impact, but still not fully be prepared for the severity of the shock and aftermath that ensues.

I often wonder where this fire in my soul comes from to let women know that not only can they do it, but that they can do it big, kick ass, and make an impact along the way. It is the flame that burns in my soul and can't be extinguished. It gets me out of bed each morning, and while writing this book, I've looked very closely at what factors in my life would have planted this seed in the beginning. While I was in the midst of my advocacy training class, a Play Therapist explained to us her therapy approach and what she does to work with children to help them best communicate their feelings. She instructed us to pick a toy off a nearby table. We were to pick out the one that spoke to us most. We then went around the room sharing why we had picked that specific toy. One lady had picked a puppy dog toy because it just looked cute and sweet. Another chose a butterfly because it was beautiful and floated around, bringing joy to everyone who witnessed it. Me… I had picked the Stretch Armstrong doll. He was wearing a red suit, sunglasses, a cheesy grin, and was striking a somewhat impressive power pose. I shared with the room I had picked him because he seemed powerful to me. Being the acutely tuned therapist she was, she took the information in, pursed her lips, narrowed her eyes, cast her gaze to the side, and asked, "Do you feel powerless or like you need more power in your life right now?" Without any hesitation whatsoever, I told her no. I felt fully powerful and empowered, but it pained me when I saw women who felt powerless. I just wanted to teach them how to own their power. I think about that class often.

When I'm seeking direction and questioning why I'm doing what I'm doing, I think about Stretch Armstrong. But it doesn't end there. I can never leave well enough alone. I have to know WHY. Why am I passionate about this? After months of seeking this question out, I believe it all goes back to my childhood. I've mentioned previously that

I was basically an enigma born into the social group I was surrounded with. For those of you that aren't aware, the religion I was raised in, at the time, didn't necessarily highlight, spotlight, or empower women. In all honesty, it was a religion that encouraged you to "let your light shine," while also teaching women to make themselves smaller, cover up, hide, and for goodness sakes, to not ever have their own opinion or voice outside of their husband or father's. It's an interesting dichotomy, and one I never truly realized was there until recently. From an early age, I recognized the fact that women had this long list of rules about what they could and couldn't do while men's list was much more flexible. Not only were women meant to be seen and not heard, but they should also cover up every inch of their body to avoid "causing a man to lust." Women needed to learn how to cook and clean and aspire to be the most supportive wife and mother they could possibly imagine. I didn't see women encouraged to dream, or God forbid, lead. Leading a women's bible study or teaching Sunday school was most I ever witnessed women leading. I yearned to see strong women of faith who had educations, careers, ministries, and businesses. I watched girls who only dreamt of marrying the perfect Christian boy (at a ridiculously young age by the way), raising perfect Christian children, dressing them in the most perfect outfits on Sunday morning, and having the pastor over for Sunday lunch. That was the Pentecostal girl's American Dream. Forget college, careers, corporate America, dreams, and financial freedom. Rich people can't go to Heaven.

I'm not saying there weren't women who led. I knew the strongest prayer warriors to walk the earth existed in my childhood. My NanNaw was one of them and the epitome of a Christian woman living a purpose-filled life with a servant's heart. She was a loving and devoted mother, grandmother, sister, daughter, and friend. But it seemed to me her purpose in life was all based upon how she served her family. I never saw her do something for herself or step out in boldness on her own. I loved her servant's heart and knew that it was exactly where she was meant to be in the body of Christ. But I wanted to know how women served others on their own terms without the label of wife, mom, daughter. Were childless single women any lesser of a part of the Kingdom? I wanted to know how I could fulfill my calling in life if I never ended up being a mother or wife. While I greatly respected the prayer warrior women around me (and God knows I needed them in my early twenties), I wanted to see women using their voices as ambassadors of truth, empowerment, and advocacy. I wanted to see women in leadership roles, living purpose-filled lives, and owning their God-given power. I wanted to see the Deborahs, Jaels, and the Rahabs. I wanted to hear a preacher say it was okay for me to step up, answer God's call, and lead, even if I didn't have a husband.

I thought for a moment back to the words my friend had shared with me about grit. I had always had a fire and known there was a great call in my life. I had always known that there was something big waiting for me to step into. What I hadn't realized was I had been through some challenges in my life. Yes, it was charmed. Yes, I had a childhood that most people would envy. But there were also trials. There were obstacles that had to be overcome. There was pain, and there was healing. There were roles and responsibilities I had taken on I hadn't needed to. And, every part of my childhood had shaped me into the person I became. It had shaped me into someone who had resilience and didn't give up.

But, if I'm telling you how I don't quit, I have to also tell you the entire story. As a result of my dad's "never give up, never give in" attitude, and being the achiever that I was, I never quit a thing growing up. Okay… piano lessons, I quit piano lessons… but I sucked! And besides, I wanted to play the drums. I was unbelievably terrible at basketball, but I showed up day in and day out for practice knowing full well I would sit on the bench until the last two minutes of the game. I worked my high school job for *six* years because I had committed to it. I never even broke up with a boyfriend because I was no quitter!

Until one day, I was, indeed, a quitter. After I had quit college and walked away from a massive scholarship, I heard the words of a mentor ring through my ears, "What a waste of a brilliant mind…" She didn't offer me any encouragement or direction. She didn't share with me how this particular college may not have been the right fit, but there were other options. She just simply wrote it off as a massive failure. After 18 years, the sting of those words still brings me to tears. I heard the words and let them infiltrate my mind. I heard her saying my mind had been wasted. And it wasn't just her; everyone said that. Everyone in my immediate circle said it. They had all had big hopes and dreams for me. I, being the achiever I was, had never before experienced the feeling of disappointing those around you. No one offered me advice or mentorship; they just expressed their disappointment with my rash decision. It was an uncomfortable position to be in. I had always been the best and done the right thing. I let that feeling of failure send me through a revolving spiral of being a quitter. I quit my high school job, and then went on to start job after job, quitting each one when things got tough. I completed Real Estate school, but never took the test. I moved in and out of apartments and houses before the leases were up. I started countless projects I never finished. I started journals knowing the pages at the back would never live their destiny of being filled with my words. But, most importantly, I quit listening to God's direction for my life.

And then, one day, I decided to quit quitting and simply put my head down, go to work, and commit to living the life of purpose that God called me to. In such, I decided to be a wife devoted to never quitting on her marriage and to constantly growing as a mother, so I would never quit my children. I committed myself to building a business I could take pride in and wouldn't want to quit. I pledged to use my voice to bring light to the dark parts of humanity and call out injustices regardless of who would tell me to quit. And, I dedicated myself to never stop seeking God's direction for my life.

The thing is, each and every one of us have our own experiences in life that have shaped us into the person we are today. I am not naive or insensitive enough to say that everything happens for a reason. I know enough peoples' hard stories to know there are some things in life that are horrifically unexplainable, and we'll never have answers to them on this side of Heaven. However, I can say every single part of my life has been a stepping-stone along the journey of my purpose. The good, the bad, and the ugly in between. It has forged me. And, I suppose, I'm a little grittier for the wear.

How to Have Grit:

1. Embrace the journey you are on as part of God's plan.

2. Be flexible, and don't expect life to fit into the box you had anticipated.

3. Have the courage to get out of your comfort zone.

4. Take the initiative to stretch and grow without waiting for anyone's permission.

5. Don't give up.

CHAPTER 7

My Mother

As I began writing this book and digging into embracing my voice, I realized it might be a great resource for understanding my mother better. My mother and I both have a gift for gab, but we speak completely different languages. I thought if I could put the story into writing, it would help me better understand her and have more patience with her. We had a strained relationship for several years, and I just needed to make it all make sense. I needed to understand what had happened and where it had all gone wrong. I wanted to find the person I knew as a child again. I wanted to find the best friend I had had as a young adult. I wanted to rekindle the relationship where we knew everything about each other and had no secrets. I wanted to find that mom who had for her children in complete and utter selfless reckless abandonment. If I could just get it on paper and out of my head, maybe it would make sense.

That mother-daughter balance beam is a tricky one. It almost makes me happy I wasn't blessed with a beautiful baby girl to dress up and adorn with bows. It seems like you hear much less often men talking about how their mothers have screwed them up. So, how do you talk about your mom in a book? The struggles? The battles? The drama? You just do it. That's how. You type it, print it, and then give it to her to read. Because she may learn those hard things, obstacles, and failures along the journey of parenting are what turned you into who you are today.

I have this morbidly weird habit. I write people's obituaries in my head. I write my own also. I think about how people will remember me, like what they will say about me. I may even write mine out at some point and put it in the safe with directions as to using it when my time comes. Weird? But I always read obituaries, the well-written ones anyway, and wonder if the person knew this about how others viewed them. Did their family ever tell them how they would remember them? Did their children thank them for the way they impacted their lives? Did they know that in spite of all the shit, they were so deeply loved? I spoke at my PawPaw's funeral and read a poem I wrote about him after his passing. To this day, I wish I would have told him those things before he was gone. I wish I would have read him the poem. I wish I would have told him all of my favorite memories with him. I find myself often wondering what I will write in my mother's obituary. I hear women talk about their complicated relationships with their mothers, and often times they mention they couldn't share the story until their mom was gone. It was too complicated. However, I choose to share now, openly, and freely, in hopes that there will be healing and peace this side of Heaven.

She has been sick all my life, so I have basically been mentally prepared to lose my mom for as long as I can remember. She has had good and bad times, and we've always navigated through. My early memories are not of my mother taking care of us but of me taking care of her and my younger brother. I don't know if I was born a nurturer or if the nature of our situation is what bred the trait. I was four when her disease hit full force. She suffers from autoimmune muscular diseases. Dermatomyositis was the earliest diagnosis. After having my brother, she never rebounded from the fatigue. Her exhaustion and muscle weakness led her to believe there was a bigger issue than just Tired Mama Syndrome. After seeing a commercial about Lupus, she went to her doctor and demanded to be tested. This was 1986, and there was very little was known about any autoimmune diseases, making the diagnosis hard to come by. She was eventually referred to a specialist that confirmed the Dermatomyositis, a part of Lupus. In the past 32 years, the diagnoses have just kept coming. Long story short, she has an autoimmune connective disease that falls under the umbrella of

Muscular Dystrophy. My parents bought our family home around the same time she was at her weakest, and my earliest memories of her are of her in bed all the time. I remember my dad shaking her into a pair of pantyhose because she was too weak to pull them up and needed to get ready for church. To this day, I can't for the life of me understand why she didn't just not wore the hose all together! Thank goodness that trend went out of style.

By the age of five, I was a pro at making scrambled eggs and bacon in the microwave for my three-year-old brother and myself. I could make coffee for my dad as well. I was never scared or worried about my mom being sick back then. At least if I was, I don't remember it. I just knew she was sick and needed someone to take care of her. Dad worked all the time to take care of our young family, and my brother was too young. So it was me who did the work, and I didn't mind. I never felt like I was being shorted in life. Then, one morning, my mother walked into the kitchen to find me standing on top of the counter, getting a bowl down from one of the top shelves. She gasped at the sight and abruptly picked me up under my arms to place me safely on the floor, telling me the whole time how that was too dangerous, and I shouldn't do it again. I didn't bother telling her it was my morning routine. I was in complete and utter awe at what just happened. I threw my arms around her waist, squeezing her as tightly as my little hands would allow and, with the joy-filled excitement, said, "You just picked me up, Momma!" It was the first time in my short life I remembered her arms being strong enough to pick me up. I knew she had when I was a baby, but that was the first time I had really experienced it. It was a milestone. It was hope. I can feel the joy in my heart to this day. I've carried it throughout my life. Looking back, I realize now that was my first realization of how badly I wanted her out of the bed and well. I wanted her to take care of me because it felt so good.

I had an amazing childhood. My parents were incredible. My mom was the "cool" mom. She did a really great job of making the most out of her good days. One such day, it was beautiful and sunny outside. She came in and told us to get our play shoes on because we were going hiking. That word sounded so strange coming out of my mother's mouth, who had not been able to get out of bed just a few days prior. We were so excited. We quickly got dressed and grabbed a thermos of black cherry Kool-Aid and some snacks for the hike. The two lots we lived on only equaled about an acre, so I was curious as to where this "hike" would take us. Little did I know, that was the day that she would teach us it was completely okay to trespass on other people's land in the name of exploration. Barbed wire fences were no match for a mom stepping on the bottom two strands while a couple of kiddos climbed through the middle to get to the other side. We crossed the pasture behind our house--which back then felt like it had to have been two miles wide, but I'm fairly sure is just a ten-acre tract. At the back of the pasture, we climbed through another barbed wire fence and picked up a cattle trail to follow. I kept asking where we were going, and she just kept telling me it was an adventure. We didn't know the destination; we were just enjoying the journey. She pointed out different types of trees, the birds along the path, and the different shapes in the clouds. We walked for what seemed like forever and were so deep in the woods, separated from all trace of civilization. As we were following the trail through cedar trees and under the canopy of tall oaks, we stumbled upon a corral. She stopped to tell us what a corral was for and how cowboys would use it to pen their cows. I started worrying we were lost and wouldn't make it back by dark. Instead of soothing my fears, she played into them, and if she knew where she was actually going, she sure had me fooled. She would check the sun to see what direction we were headed in and go by to try to make our way back to the house. However, her calculations must have been off. Rather than making our way back to the house, we stumbled upon what every kid in our neighborhood would recall as being the single greatest place to spend countless hours of childhood. As we were walking, she stopped us in our tracks, holding her finger to her lips and shushing us. I was already nervous and anxious to get back before the sun set, so this did not settle my nerves.

"Shh... Do you hear that?" Oh man, I thought... This is it. We were gonna die.

"What?" I asked timidly.

"Water. I hear water. Let's keep walking." And, by gosh! That cattle trail had led us to the most amazing playground we could have never dreamt up. The creek wound its way through these trees and led to destinations that entertained our imagination for hours. The hike led us to discover our favorite past time, and the journey to get there was half the adventure. With our friends, we beat a path crossing the ditch in my backyard, climbing through the barbed wire fence, hiking across the pasture, dodging cow patties and snakes, climbing over yet another barbed wire fence, and weaving our way through the trees, following shaded beaten cattle trails. The creek seemed to always be running, so as you approached, you could hear the water trickling downstream before it actually made an appearance. The sun shone down through breaks in the tree branches overhead, and you could sit mesmerized with the rays dancing on the water indefinitely. By some unknown act of nature, the red clay soil that surrounded my property transformed into a white sandy beach that lined each side of the creek. Vines dropped down from overhead branches created the perfect jungle gym opportunity to grab one and swing across the creek. The red clay embankment on the opposite side of the creek was steep and scattered with rocks and vines that made for perfect hand and footholds to scale the embankment. Countless hours were spent in that creek, running, splashing, laughing with friends, dreaming up stories, imagining our futures, and just being kids-- young, wild, and free. And to think, we would have never known this haven existed had my mother not taken us hiking to explore our surroundings.

She sounds amazing, doesn't she? All my friends loved her. I had the cool mom. She would throw lavish birthday parties. By lavish, I mean all our friends could stay the night, and we would have a homemade birthday cake, light a bonfire, and grill hot dogs. She would take us on hayrides, tell us ghost stories, let us freeze each other's underwear, and toilet paper the neighbor's house. Every time, the same poor neighbor... When we got older and had questions about sex, my mom was the one we all went to. Nothing was off-limits and, while she gave us plenty of rules, she kept an open dialogue with us. All of my childhood (and adult) friends have fond memories of her. So, one would assume a strained relationship as adults would not have ever been a possibility in this mother-daughter fairy tale. I don't really know when it happened. I don't know when I started resenting her, or when she started competing with me. I have been able to see things more clearly by writing this book, and no one is really right or wrong. We're just both people dealing with our own crap. Growing up, we had a great relationship. And I stated that correctly. We grew up together. She was barely 19 when I was born, and we literally grew up together. There were times we behaved, and argued, more like sisters rather than mother and daughter. This was the dynamic of our relationship, and it wasn't until I had children of my own I realized I wanted a different dynamic. At one point in time, she was my best friend, and we shared no secrets. I miss that time desperately. It was that period of time between childhood and full-blown adulthood. It was a time where her children were grown and out of the house, and I had yet to start a family. It was a time where we were able to see each other as women, not as mother and daughter. Just as two women who enjoyed each other's company and had a mutual respect for one another. My mom was always my biggest fan. She was so proud of me each and every time I achieved something, won an award, or accomplished a great feat. She would brag relentlessly about me to her friends. However, at some point, the bragging was replaced by something else I couldn't quite name.

I can only speak to what it feels like for me in hopes it helps someone else going through something similar. Because her story is her own to share, I can only say that from my perspective, my mom struggles with insecurity and lacking self-confidence. She was determined to raise a confident daughter who knew her worth. I am forever grateful she gave her all to this mission and succeeded. However, when I developed into an adult, it seemed to be something she almost resented. Mother-daughter relationships are just sticky and messy as best I can tell. Even in the most Christ-filled relationships, I see the same struggles. I hear women talk about this frequently, and I always think, if we could just have this conversation with our mothers, we might be able to break free of these strongholds. I have no idea why we have yet to learn how to smoothly navigate this dynamic.

If my mother has said it once, I've heard it a thousand times:

"I always wanted to raise a confident daughter, but I didn't mean to do that good of a job." She means no harm by it and says it in jest, but every single time, it stings. Why would she resent me for being confident? Is being confident a bad trait? Why wouldn't she just be proud of the daughter she raised? At first, I would think maybe I was too confident and needed to reel myself in. But the more I would lean into it, the more God would assure me He made me this way. The more I questioned God about the competitive feeling of the remarks, the more He assured me those comments were not about me. They were simply her own inner dialogue. And He would remind me my validation lies in Him. Just like it doesn't come from my friends, family, or husband, it also doesn't come from my mother. I can now hear those statements and dismiss them, knowing she truly means no malice by them. I can pray she feels nothing more than love from me.

I have to speak to my resentment issues as well. It wasn't clear until I sat down and began writing and documenting this entire journey that it came together for me. Throughout my life, people have told me that I look like my mother or remind them of her, and I'm quick to respond that while I look like my mom, I act like my dad. I never wanted to be like her. I empathized with her, but I didn't want to be her. I saw her physically ill and weak most of my childhood, and I wanted so badly for her to be strong. I didn't want to be like her because it would be the opposite of being strong. I recognize recently the underlying reason I have such a passion for empowering women and helping them realize their strengths is because I so badly wanted my mom to be strong as a little girl. I wanted her to just stand up and say her disease didn't define her. I couldn't make her strong, and that is why I have the innate desire to help other women realize their strength. I saw my dad as the epitome of strength. He could work outside all day, come home late, and wrestle with us in the floor or play baseball in the front yard. He worked hard, made money, and got things done. He was tough, and I wanted to be like him. I wanted to be strong.

Here's where I have to give credit to the Enneagram! I am a three-wing-two. If you're new to the Enneagram, you have no idea what I'm talking about right now. Go take a free enneagram test. The Enneagram is a nine-point personality system that combines psychology and traditional wisdom to help better understand why we are the way we are and how we interact with others. My label means this:

> 3: "The Achiever" Self-assured, highly driven for advancement, ambitious, competent. They pursue success and want to be admired.

> 2: "The Helper" Feeling-based with a focus on relationships. They are great at connecting with people, empathizing with others, serving, and bringing out other's potential.

I have no degree in this department, but I have done enough self-discovery as well as "research" on this topic to realize I most likely get my three-ness from my dad and my two-ness from my mom. Disclaimer, I don't know their numbers. But I would put a hefty wager on those being their numbers.

That's the crazy part of the miracle of life and two people coming together to form another human being with their DNA and genetic markers. The baby is born, the family gathers around, and people start commenting. The mom's family exclaims she got her mother's eyes. The dad's family cries out she has his chin. They both agree the lips and mouth are a nice combination of the two of them. But you don't get to see the personality characteristics that come from each side until later. When a child acts up, you'll hear a parent grumble to the other parent that "their child" needs to be disciplined. With my two boys, we would find ourselves saying our oldest had gotten all the good qualities from both of us, and our younger one, in all his stubborn defiance, had gotten all of our combined less than desired traits. However, the truth is both of our children ended up with an amazing blend of both of our personalities. The youngest just simply inherited very strong leadership skills, and can sometimes prove to be a challenge. He's going to be a leader who does great things in life; we just have to say a prayer for patience along the way.

I personally think I, too, inherited both of my parents' absolute best qualities. While my mother wasn't the epitome of outward strength I wanted to see in my life, she was the one who taught me compassion. She taught me selflessness and the importance of serving others. She taught me to take up for the underdog and look out for the outlier. She taught me to seek good in everyone, and most importantly, she taught me to always know that what you see on the surface does not tell you what a person has been through. She taught me that I don't know anyone's story until they choose to share it with me. She taught me not to judge a book by its cover because it doesn't matter what a person looks like; what matters is their heart. She taught me to share my light with everyone who came along, and she taught me the most important lesson of all, to not only love the marginalized, but serve them as well. So yes, I have my mother's physical features. But I also have her servant's heart and will proudly don that any day.

How to Have A Healthy-Ish Relationship with Your Mother:

1. Accept your mother as a flawed human being just like yourself and extend grace.

2. Remember your validation comes from your Creator and not your mother's opinion of you.

3. Identify what positive traits of your mother's were passed down to you. Thank her and God for those gifts.

4. Know that in Heaven, we will all speak the same language, and there will be no struggles of communication.

CHAPTER 8

A Conversation with my 19-Year-Old Self...

At 19 years old, my mother became my mother. She was a baby with a baby. I remember nineteen as being one of the most confusing times of my life. I remember struggling with failure and disappointment. I remember experiencing plans being shattered. I remember processing true heartbreak for the first time. I remember grieving the loss of a loved one. I remember turning to unhealthy coping mechanisms. I remember knowing there was a big call on my life and no clue how to fulfill it. I remember the utterly lost feeling. If I could, I would go back and let 19-year-old me know how life turned out. She was a bit of a hot mess back then and could have really used a mentor to speak into her. So, if you will, oblige me for a bit while I tell her she's going to be okay:

Dear 19-year-old me:

It's going to be okay. Trust the process. God has this beautifully designed plan for your life. I know, I know, you've heard that before. But, trust me. Your mom, and grandma, and aunts, and teachers are right. God is in control, and His plan is so much better than you could ever imagine. I know that you have big plans in life. I know that you freak out when things don't go according to that plan. But it's okay. He's got you.

That boy that just broke your heart. The one that your parents warned you about, the one you planned on marrying one day if you ever slowed down from your college and career goals. Let him go. I know it hurts. I know you gave him a piece of your heart and trusted him with it, but it's okay. God has something so much better for you. God is going to bring someone into your life who not only makes your heart race, but is so supportive and loving to the core. You will lie awake at night, staring at his face thinking how lucky you are to have married your best friend. Your love will grow so great for each other. You'll hope and pray you get to know each other as husband and wife in Heaven because you can't imagine ever being without him. This man will love you so deeply you would never question his intentions or love for you. This man will encourage you, support you, stand beside you, lead you when you are weak, and let you lead when he is. He will listen to you, dream with you, and understand everything about you to your very core. He'll look at you with eyes that are full of adoration, respect, and endless love. You'll feel him stare into your heart each and every time. When it feels like you are alone on an island and the entire world is attacking you, he will gladly stand on that island with you. He will pull his sword and go to battle for you against anyone and anything that comes against you. He will not just have your back. He will stand in the fire with you. He will brave the battle as long as he knows you are by his side. He will stand in the shadows and silently support you in every situation. Regardless of how many people may be in a room or how far apart you may be from one another, you can lock eyes across the crowd and have a full conversation that lets you know you are the most beautiful and amazing woman he has ever met. His arms will be the safest, warmest, most comfortable place you've ever laid. His embrace will be your favorite place on earth. You and he will grow deeper in love each and every day for as many days as God blesses you with on this earth. You'll live by the motto that a man doesn't make you strong, but the right partner makes you stronger.

Those people you've met at college who don't look like you, believe the same as you, or sound like you, it's okay. You can be friends with them. You can even love them. You're going to make many new friends over the next 18 years. They are going to come in all shapes, sizes, colors, and beliefs. You get to embrace and befriend every single one of them. You even get to love them. You learn from them. You become stronger in your faith by having them in your life. You get to extend love and grace to them. There will be a day when your circle of friends doesn't look like only white, middle class, Republican, Southern Christians. There will be a day where more of your friends have criminal records than don't. Because of your friends, you get to learn how Jesus loves us both horizontally and vertically. You get to be in relation with Jesus and then share his love with all of his people, not just the ones that look and sound like you. You get to share Jesus with your new friends and your old friends. You get to learn Jesus can live inside of each and every one of us whether we look the part or not. You get to learn from your new friends and become a better person because of them.

That diet of ramen noodles, raviolis, chocolate milk, pickles, and Dr. Peppers… It has to go. Don't worry though; you become quite the culinary connoisseur. And, I hate to break it to you, but you break up with Dr. Peppers… I'm not saying you won't ever have a sip of that sinfully sweet, syrupy nectar of the gods ever again, but you refrain from it 99.5% of the time. However, you do have moments of weakness. Typically in the middle of Summer, when it's too hot for coffee, and you're just craving something cool and sweet that packs a punch! Oh coffee… yeah, you haven't given that up yet. You still like it black, and still carry around an enormously large mug the size of your head, sipping on it until lunchtime or later. There is this incredible new invention that has completely changed your coffee game! It's a Yeti mug! It stays hot the entire time you're sipping on it! There's no need to go back to the dorm to microwave the bottom half of the coffee. As for Raviolis… more disappointing news. The last time you tried to eat them was over a decade ago. And, for some reason, that once delightful meat filling in the center now tastes like and resembles canned dog food. You just can't do it. As for the ramen, yeah, it got kicked to the curb along with its other friends. It's not a taste thing; it still smells amazing anytime you smell someone nuking a bowl, like your teenage son who buys it and hides a secret stash. But, the copious amounts of preservatives, chemicals, and MSG went entirely against your moral fiber. When you do enjoy a piping hot bowl of ramen nowadays, it's made with Organic, gluten-free rice noodles and scrumptious bone broth. Bone broth, you ask? I know, you've never heard of it. It's delicious and has so many amazing immune-boosting properties. I swear it's one of the main reasons your kids are healthy as horses! Kids? I'll get to that later.

Take a breath, don't hyperventilate. It works out fine. Kids are not nearly as terrible as you had imagined. They're actually pretty cool, and you've managed to keep them alive thus far. Chocolate milk has a whole different look to it in your fridge now. The milk comes from a local dairy and is raw milk, unpasteurized. When there is time, you make the chocolate syrup from scratch. The kids love it! Yes, kids. I'll get there. Although you still love the delicious creamy sweetness of the chocolate milk, you don't drink it because you don't do sugar anymore really… only in extremely limited quantities on rare occasions. And dairy is the culprit for those breakouts you keep getting, so we get rid of that too. Powdered donuts… That breakfast has been replaced by a nutritious protein bar. You totally did not get rid of your pickles, though! You still have at least one a day. They're not going anywhere. You eat a mostly organic diet and have for the past 14 years, ever since you got pregnant with your oldest.

Okay, I guess it's time we talk about the kids. Yes, I remember you had big career plans. I know. Undergrad in International Studies with a Sociology minor and an emphasis in Spanish. Two years in the Peace Corps. Grad school at Johns Hopkins SAIS, followed by an internship on the Hill, and an international career, foreign service, ambassadorship, etc… I know. I know there would be no time for kids. I remember.

At twenty-three years old, you found yourself lucky enough to have found the love of your life. Specifically, that guy I was talking about up there. You were lucky enough to be friends with him for a couple of years before the two of you decided to have a relationship. So, you knew each other really well and had shared a lot of laughs by the time you were together. You also knew his plans for the future as well as your own. Neither of you really ever planned to get re-married or have any (more) kids. You have a stepson. He was ten when you met him. He's super cool. None of those horrific step-mom-step-kid stories you hear about. He's grown now and is married. He is an amazing human being. A massive blessing! Your relationship with him is one of the things you're most grateful for in life. He is an awesome role model for your little boys. You have two others. Both boys. Yeah, I know. Totally lucked out on that one. I mean, have you met a teenage girl lately?

So anyway, there you were, in this relationship with the love of your life. You were best friends & having so much fun together. You had a sneaking suspicion neither one of you was going to get out of this relationship inside of this lifetime. You spent the days fishing, traveling, and hanging out with friends. And then, it happened. You were going to have a baby. Yeah! I know! Yes, you had to tell NanNaw. It's okay though! She didn't disown you, and you're still just as close. Closer even. Not the easiest thing to go through. But, remember how I told you about His plan? He knew exactly what He was doing, and He needed to save both you and that amazing man from yourselves. You guys were meant to be a family and spend the rest of your lives together. Remember, God does not make mistakes.

Not going to lie, you were terrified for the entire pregnancy. I mean, you actually enjoyed every single second of being pregnant. Since you had never really planned to have kids, you did what you do best-- you educated yourself. I can't even tell you how many books you read. You had decided that if you were doing this, you were going to do it well. At one point, your doctor told you to quit reading books about what to expect when expecting and start reading books about what to do when the kid gets there. In the first few days after you brought him home, you, your stepson, and your husband stood around the bassinet just staring at his beautiful little face while he slept. You just sat there thinking how unbelievable it was you could have so much overwhelming love for a person you just met. While you were deep in thought about the miracle of life, your stepson popped up with, "So, we just stand here and watch him sleep? Is that how it works?" And, at that point, you realized that you didn't have to know it all raising kids; you would just learn as you go. Oh, and that little boy...? He is amazing! He loves his Mama so much. He's taller than you now. And the little stinker is good at every single thing he tries! It's kind of annoying. He's this incredible athlete. That's the coolest thing about kids. They're these incredible individuals with their own talents and skills that you get to sit back and watch develop.

I told you, it's not nearly as awful as what you had imagined. Actually, you ended up loving it! It felt like the best job you had ever had, and you wanted more. You wanted lots more. You loved having and raising babies. You and your husband went back and forth about this for about 18 months. You wanted another baby, and you really wanted a little girl. And then, your sweet baby turned about 17 months and was the most active, curious little stinker ever, and you decided you were fine with just the one. He was plenty to keep up with. You dropped it and moved on with life. Until, one day, a few months later, your husband walked in the door and informed you that you guys should have another baby so your son would have a playmate. You, of course, said okay and hoped and prayed for a little girl. You even followed the book "How to Choose the Sex of your Baby." You dreamt of your little girl and had all these amazing girl names until you went for the sonogram and found out she had a penis. You asked your doctor what on earth you were going to do with two boys, and she told you it was going to be great. They were going to love each other, be playmates, and have a best friend for life. And, she was right.

Being a boy mom is the coolest thing ever. You get to spend your days watching baseball, basketball, and football games. You spend weekends at dirt bike races, which is your absolute most favorite form of family time. Dad is the coach, and it's an entire day of forced family fun! You *love* it! Your kids take after their daddy and can ride anything with wheels. Your little one is quite possibly the cutest child to ever walk the face of the planet. He's just as every bit as stubborn and hard-headed as you, your dad, and PawPaw... not to mention his daddy as well. Poor kid, he didn't stand a chance. He did, however, inherit the natural-born leadership skills both you and your husband possess, and I know he will do great things in life. He's a deep thinker and has a huge heart. His love language is gifts, and he loves spoiling others with them. He's hilarious as well! He was born 40 years old, and kids have always annoyed him. Sound familiar? He's incredibly business-minded and drawn to purpose and helping others. I couldn't wait to see what he does with his life.

So yeah, you took ten years off from everything else in life and focused on staying home with these boys. You make healthy fresh breakfasts for them almost every morning and pack their lunches still. However, at 13 & 10, they've started mostly packing their own lunches while you oversee or edit the contents. You've spent countless hours homeschooling them for Pre-K, volunteering as class mom, taking snacks (all homemade and organic) to their class parties, riding along on field trips, volunteering as cub scout leader, and teaching Sunday school.

Oh college, and career? You want to know what happened there? Well, remember how you've always been incredibly driven? What did that counselor in high school diagnose you as? Oh yeah, Type A, OCD, perfectionist… yeah, about that. Turns out, while you were always encouraged to follow your dreams and chase your goals, someone should have taught you about self-care. I mean, I don't know if you would have listened or not, but turns out, you can't run 90 to nothing, burning the candle at both ends, without taking time to get your mind, body, and soul right. You can't run around pouring from an empty cup. So, you know how you're taking 20 hours of classes, interning 10 hours a week, working on campus 15 hours a week, and off campus 20+ hours? Well, apparently, you're destined for a burnout… sooner rather than later actually. You end up freaking out, dropping out of college, and walking away from a really large scholarship. This following that breakup you just went through. And then, right after dropping out of college, the nation was rocked by the first terrorist attack on US soil since Pearl Harbor.

You watched your country go to war with an unknown enemy in an unknown location. You yearned for justice for the 2,996 people that senselessly died at the hands of evil terrorists while at the same time doubting this was the way to handle it. Certainly, the bad guys needed to be brought to justice, but it seemed like there may have been a lot of unnecessary harm and devastation done to innocent bystanders. You watched people stereotype and classify every single Muslim as a terrorist, but knew this couldn't be true because you had just spent time closely with so many good ones on your college campus. You knew that you couldn't judge an entire culture of people based on some bad ones. You reminded friends and family that the OKC bombing was a white American, but they weren't having it. You watched fear grip the entire nation and let fear grip you as well. You became scared of flying. I know, you can't even imagine it. You love flying so much. You slept like a baby on a plane before you watched four planes full of men, women, and children, be highjacked by men wielding box cutters, and flown into buildings filled with men, women, and children. You yearned so deeply for justice and protection but wished for war-free conflict resolution. Remember how you prayed as a little girl during the Gulf War that there would be no more war, and people could solve problems without bombs and killing people? You ended up praying that same prayer again at 19, 20, 21, 22… The whole experience left you questioning the political system, people as a whole, and feeling grateful that you had avoided the career path you had formerly planned for. However, that didn't take your passion for people away or your desire to do big things on a big scale.

It's okay that you quit college. You felt like a huge failure, but it's okay. It worked out great. Just wait and see. Remember that whole God's plan thing. He's got you. I know you felt like a huge failure. I know this was your first experience with failure. I know that you felt like you let your family down, your teachers down, your professors down, the scholarship donors down. I know that. I remember you were voted Most Likely to Succeed. You were going to be the first female president, or something like that. But, sit tight. It gets good. I know you never intended to be a stay at home mom, but man you rocked it! You had that Mom game wrapped up! Still do, if I do say so myself. Remember that perfect idea you had of a house perched on a cliff overlooking the water where you could sit and write, gazing out at the water? You're sitting in it right now. You're watching the rain fall, listening to it drip off the gutters, while you watch the drops splatter across the lake. You're in your dream home. It's not in Hawaii, but it's pretty darn close! You have an incredible husband who busted his tail and took care of you for those ten years that you stayed home with kiddos. You never wanted for anything. You carried all the nice handbags and went on all the once in a lifetime vacations.

But something was missing. You knew there was something else. You knew there was something bigger. You just couldn't get out of your own head and see it didn't have to look like what you had envisioned. It doesn't look like your previous plan, but you do fulfill your purpose. You now use your voice to speak into others, empower, and inspire. You have a successful business, mentor trafficked survivors, inspire women to own their power and follow their purpose, and you contribute to fighting injustices at a global level. You did alright kid. As it turns out, quitting college didn't take your purpose away from you. *You* took your purpose away from yourself. But, thank goodness God didn't give up on you.

So, dear 19-year-old me. Take a deep breath. It's going to be okay. God's got you!

Divine Design

While en route to Taos, New Mexico for a week of snow skiing with my family and reading a book on leadership, social-media, and self-awareness, purpose was something I had been struggling with. I had known all my life I had a greater purpose. I knew all my life that I was destined for greatness. The kind that would not only leave an impact but impact me as well. As I was reading that book, somewhere on the page, those words began to spell out my purpose.

"I know what my purpose is!" I all but shouted to my husband, who was trying to navigate the windy, snow-covered road on an uphill climb. "I'm supposed to be speaking to people. Like, large crowds of people."

"Yeah, babe, you already do that," he responded without taking his eyes off the road.

"No, I know. But I'm supposed to be speaking to people about something else. Not just skincare, but something else, too. Like, something bigger. Skincare's great! But, there's something else. I think I need to be speaking into people and empowering them."

"And, how exactly do you plan to fit that into your schedule with all you have going on?" His eyes cut over to me and he breathed out a breath that I believe was his recognition of increased household duties he saw in his near future.

"I'll just get a bigger plate. It's okay. Trust me. I just have to figure it out."

To this day, when we start that uphill climb on the way to the ski resort, my husband looks across the vehicle and reminds me that this is where I found my purpose.

April 21, 2017: *SUCCESS Live conference*

That conference was the first time I heard Mel Robbins speak. In all actuality, I'm not sure I knew who Mel Robbins was before that day. I was instantly mesmerized the second she came out wearing a colorful floral printed flowy skirt, black button-down dress shirt, and sparkly tennis shoes. Her energy was electric. I could feel my heart pounding. There might as well have only been the two of us in the room. She was speaking straight to me. And then she talked about the 5 Second Rule. This was so similar to a training I had done a few months earlier focusing on CAN.

Nothing, and I mean absolutely nothing, gets my blood boiling like someone telling me they can't do something. (I actually wanted to name this book "C*nt is a bad word." But I figured my Christian audience might be turned off by that title.) It literally makes me angry to hear a person have such a limited mindset, and it's one of the most common phrases I hear in my line of work.

I had a mentee at the aftercare home tell me she couldn't create the vocational plan she wanted. "I can't do it. It's going to take too long, and I don't have enough time." This attitude annoys me anytime, but when it's coming from someone who has had their power taken from them and their dreams stolen, I get really fired up! She had been so excited the first day of class, sharing her dreams with me, and now she was dejected and didn't believe she could even let herself stretch towards that goal because of that single, four-letter word. I saw the disappointment in her eyes. I saw the limited mindset creep in. I saw her hear the words of some douchebag from her past who had told her she couldn't do something… and my blood began to boil.

I pushed all class materials to the side and made her look me in the eye. I had her repeat her dreams to me without any objections or excuses. I reiterated the fact that while we may have had limited resources in the past, that does not define our present or determine our future. I explained to her the importance of never giving up on those dreams. I encouraged her to focus, not on the big goal she believed she couldn't do, but on the one thing she *can* do to get one step closer. By the end of the class, I could see her shoulders lighten and demeanor soften. I could see a glimmer of hope she might allow herself to stretch for her dreams. As much as I was fired up, I have to laugh, because as the rest of the class watched the encounter, one of the girls said, "Mrs. Brandi, you was sweating and throwing your jacket off! I thought you was ready to fight." And, she was correct, I am willing to fight to help any woman anywhere realize what she is truly capable of.

I had trained the CAN effect for a few years by the time I had my blood boiling in class at the aftercare home. This is when you find yourself believing that you can't do something. Instead of listening to that voice, you immediately stop and CAN: Cognitively Assess the Now. In other words, when you think you can't do something because it seems too big or grandiose or causes you anxiety, take a breath and think about what you CAN do in that exact moment. This is a practice I have been inadvertently applying to my life for quite some time, and I finally gave it a name. In business, I coach people to quit saying they can't and simply figure out how to CAN. At home, my family doesn't catch a break either. My husband and kids are constantly being told to come from a place of yes and know I am not interested in hearing whatever it is that they think they "can't" do. They know the quickest way to irritate me is to tell me something that can't be done. Don't tell me you can't; figure out how you can.

When my youngest was about to start school, I kept thinking, "I can't believe my baby is starting school, and there's nothing I can do to stop it!" This only led to anxiety and eventually, full-blown panic attacks. It was out of my control… But what could I control? I could clean out his closet and dresser, arrange his clothes, and have him set up for success. That way, the waking up early, fighting over what to wear, and leaving mom while he spent the day with strangers struggle would be replaced with him being able to gain independence and get dressed on his own. I firmly believe the perspective from which we view things can actually change the things we view. When you change the way you see obstacles, you make room for opportunity. These are some simple examples of how anyone can apply the CAN approach to life.

- I CAN'T lose weight. I CAN choose to not eat junk food today.

- I CAN'T get out of debt. I CAN write out a budget today.

- I CAN'T run a mile. I CAN walk half a mile today.

- I CAN'T speak in front of a crowd. I CAN speak in front of my mirror today.

- I CAN'T reach that many people. I CAN meet one new person today.

- I CAN'T change the world. I CAN serve where I am today.

With her 5 Second Rule, Mel had the same can-do brutally truthful approach at life as I did. I was amazed! I instantly thought to myself, "This. This is what I should be doing in life. There need to be more people like us who can go out and speak into others without sugar-coating it or telling them everything was okay!" The world needed more women who would serve as accountability partners for those who were making excuses. Before Mel, I hadn't seen women in that arena. I didn't even know what that arena really looked like. Sure, I had seen females speak and heard similar messages, but this? This was different. This was exactly what I felt called to. This was my purpose. I just had to figure out the implementation of it. Before the conference was over, we were instructed to write down, "This is the year that I ____." Desperate to fully discover my purpose, I thought about it for a moment and immediately felt the pull of my international studies heart. I quickly completed the sentence, "take a mission trip to Africa."

November 2017: *A Group Chat with A Close Friend*

"Hey, I think I want to put on a leadership retreat. We'll focus on self-care, personal development, and discovering your purpose. I just think that more women need to hear this message, and I think we need to make a weekend out of it. Since you're a counselor, do you want to do this with me?" In true ride or die nature, Heather responded with "Hell Yes! *When* are we doing this?"

February 8, 2018: *The Power Project Retreat at Wildcatter Ranch*

A group of women traveled from multiple states and hundreds of miles to assemble on a luxury dude ranch in the middle of nowhere. We didn't know each other, and there wasn't one person who had ever met all of the women before this retreat. We kicked the retreat off with a meticulously prepared meal in a private dining room and shared stories and laughter, tears and heartache, and prayed for each other around the table. From an outsider's perspective, this assembly of strangers looked like we had been friends forever. We all bunked up in a room after dinner, sharing more laughter, and giving ourselves facials.

We woke up the next morning to freezing temperatures... 17 degrees. This was a stark contrast to the high sixties we had walked back from dinner in the night before. After sprinting through the needle-like wind to the main building, and feasting on a perfectly arrayed breakfast spread, we made our way to the conference room where my friend Megan led us in Holy Yoga. Anyone who knows me knows Yoga is vital to my sanity. My mind runs at 100 mph in 1.15 billion different directions at all times. Therefore, it's inevitable I forget to breathe occasionally. I forget to stop and check in with my body. This results in a neurotic headspace of anxiety and stress. So, I go to yoga minimally once a week, preferably twice a week, and practice at home. But the class is vital. I need someone to tell me to breathe. I wanted to show these women, most of whom had never practiced yoga before, how it can be used as a tool to not only decompress, clarify your thoughts, and control anxiety, but also allow you to listen to God.

Following the yoga session, Heather jumped into self-care, teaching the group the importance of first filling your cup before you could be helpful to anyone else. My friend Kayla, a personal coach, focusing on strategic intervention, followed her with a session on living a life of design and not default. I wrapped the day up with a presentation on embracing your God-given power and living a purpose-filled life. I shared in this session how so often we feel like we have to tidy everything up and make it look nice before we can answer God's call. I admitted my own doubts, fears, and hesitations. There, at the front of the conference room, I shared with the group how I wasn't sure I should be speaking about God when I occasionally drink too much red wine and sometimes drop an F-bomb. And, that was the moment. That was when she spoke the words I needed to hear. The girl in the back corner. The one who had only spoken to her sister the entire time. The one that didn't know anyone else in the room. The one that I was hoping didn't feel like she had totally wasted her money coming to the retreat. She instantly interrupted and said, "No, that is exactly why you should be standing up there speaking about God. I believe you. You're not pretending to be someone else or being fake. You're real. I'm listening to what you're saying because you're not trying to make it look all perfect." That was when I knew I was walking in faith. That was when I knew that even though I am prone to a foul mouth, I can still do God's work. I'm flawed but forgiven. That was the push I needed to share my vision with more people.

How to Take The First Steps on Your Purpose Journey:

1. Whatever call you feel on your heart, write it down.

2. Research to find out what it will take to achieve that goal.

3. Take steps to bring that goal to fruition.

Bish Stole My Book...

After getting kids off to school one morning, I sat down with a cup of coffee, did my morning devotional, and then checked out social media. Facebook informed me it was International Women's Day. My wheels started spinning; I needed to come up with an angle. I should make a post about the inspiring women in my life. I started thinking about the women around me who were empowered. These are the women I had craved to see when I was younger. I suddenly realized I had a wealth of women living purpose-filled lives all around me. I thought, maybe instead of a post, I should do interviews. I could do multiple interviews throughout the day, highlighting women who were empowering and inspiring to other women. I had created The Power Project page on Facebook five days before, so this would be a great platform to jump off of. In my mind, I had thought the page would be a space for my friends and me to host virtual retreats and trainings. It was the easy way to reach the masses, so I could use it to spotlight these women in a "vlog-like" setting. Since I'm not only an achiever but also an activator, I tend to act quickly after having an idea. I immediately reached out to a handful of women to see who could do a live interview with me that day. Alicia Bush of Treasured Vessels, whom I had never met in person, was the first one who said she would be thrilled to help me out, and we set a time for later that afternoon.

That morning I posted, "Happy #internationalwomensday. At the Power Project, POWER stands for: Purpose, Ownership, Wisdom,

Empowerment, and Reach. However, today, we're switching it up and putting #WOMEN at the center of power. We're not talking about 'beat your chest and say you're better than men kind of power.' We're talking about a God-given power that has been instilled upon you that should you choose to say yes, you can channel and go out to change the world. And, too many of us are too busy trying to hide our own power in order to not offend or make someone feel less than… That someone being our girlfriends who we're afraid of what they might think of us. Or, our husbands, because we're afraid of damaging their masculinity by embracing our power. But what society is not telling us is that we were meant to be powerful. We were made to be Deborah's, and no one talks about Deborah."

Deborah was a prophetess in the Bible who led armies of men to greatness. She was very different from the meek, humble, and submissive version of a Christian woman I had heard preached about from the pulpit. In 36 years, I had never heard of Deborah, until a friend pointed out I had a Deborah anointing. I had no clue what she meant until I read Deborah's story for myself. My mind was blown! She was the first time I had seen a female character in the Bible I truly connected to. How sad is it I had been on a church pew since I was born and had never heard the story of Deborah & Jael?

I went on to interview Alicia that day on The Power Project and had a great response to the message. She's a woman with a purpose and tenaciously seeks after God's own heart. You could read all about it in her book, *Tenacious*.

8:35 PM March 8: Text conversation with a friend from church. Friend sends picture of *Girl Wash Your Face*.

> Friend: You need to read this book. I follow her socials and finished the book a few days ago. Now I'm reading it again and highlighting and taking notes like crazy! She reminds me of you a lot!

> Me: Are you the one that told me about this? If not, someone else has told me the same thing.

Friend: I've talked about it to several people and posted about it. Not really sure who I've talked to about it. I'm not a big reader like I used to be, but this book drew me in. She's the reason for the hour early wake-up workouts, and I'm working in other changes. I just shared a video she posted about fighting against what brings you down. For her, its anxiety. For me, it's laziness and apathy.

Me: I've battled that anxiety monster… and I promise you that yoga and meditation combined with giving God the control is what cured me! It sneaks in every now and then, and that's when I know that I need to go take an hour to do some yoga, be still, be quiet, and be in God's presence. I really think it was someone else that told me about her. I think I may start a book study on The Power Project page. I love books featured on personal development and primarily empowerment. People recommend books quite a bit.

Friend: That's what she said in her video. When she feels anxiety creeping in, she knows what she has to do, and she just gets up and does it!! I could try to do some book studies. Like I said, I haven't been an avid reader for several years, but I do like to buy them and start them, but I never finish them. It's kind of an addiction! I was worried I was throwing away money, again, buying this book. So glad I did it without questioning myself. Good night sweet friend! 4:30 will be here before I know it!

March 11, 2018: Message conversation with another friend:

Friend: I want to do something super fun with this book, *Girl Wash Your Face* for the women in our surrounding communities. And, I think it would be super fun to do it with you, especially considering the title and the connection with your skincare business. Not sure exactly what or when but if you are interested, let me know. The author is currently doing an online book club over it. This is how she broke it down.

March 29, 2018: I finished *Girl Wash Your Face.*

I couldn't stop this book! I listened with bated breath, on the edge of my seat for the duration of the seven hours and four minutes of everything I've ever wanted to say in a book! She was me! My voice was hers! We were destined to become best friends! I was raised Pentecostal, and so was she. I was a good girl in high school. She was a good girl in high school. I'm short. She's short. I like to write. She likes to write. I tell people to wash their faces. She tells people to wash their faces. I am brutally truthful. She is brutally truthful. I want to encourage people to be the best version of themselves. She wants people to be the best version of themselves. See where this is going? Yup, straight into Full Blown Stalker tendencies. I immediately subscribed to her podcast, and over the course of a few days, listened to every single episode. I legitimately stalked her on every form of social media. I watched every piece of media she had ever shot until my head was so dang full of inspiration and empowerment it could explode. Finally! There was someone like me! There was an outspoken, Christian woman not afraid to hustle, work hard, chase dreams, and tell others to quit making excuses. I took out a pen and made a journal entry:

> "I have just shared the stage with Rachel Hollis! It was incredible. The house was packed, and we poured into everyone there! Lives were changed. The electricity in the room was incomparable! I will never forget the feeling of this accomplishment in this moment."

This was how I had written my dreams down for years. I actually found a journal from my freshman year at college, and as I looked back over the list of my 18-year-old goals, I could not believe how many I accomplished. It's amazing what writing your dreams into existence can do for your personal motivation to chase those goals.

April 8: Started an eight-week virtual book study on *Girl Wash your Face* on The Power Project Facebook page.

April 10: I direct messaged Ms. Rachel Hollis because I couldn't take it anymore.

> Me: Okay, I have to ask because I have my entire team as well as the majority of our company reading your book right now. Are you a consultant with my skincare company? You literally took my three most favorite things and combined them in a book: personal development, washing your face, and girl power! Rock on Sister!

> Rachel: Hey Brandi girl! I am not a consultant but so glad that you are enjoying the book!

> Me: Lol! I had a luncheon yesterday where I was shamelessly plugging your book beforehand and where people were asking the question. Our corporate field director even had it in her bag. I told them I'd get to the bottom of it. Love it! I'm also putting a request in for you as keynote speaker at convention!

> Rach: "You are so sweet, and I would LOVE that! You can send any info over to my assistant!

This happens to be one of my superpowers. I have the ability to see people as people, and no one is off limits to me. Everyone, and I mean everyone, is fully approachable for me. Thank you, social media, for making this far more possible than the old days where I had to write letters to everyone. Now, I could just shoot my pal Rach a DM. Listen, I am completely aware that this message exchange was most likely the result of a very sweet and approachable assistant. I just appreciate actual conversational exchanges on social media.

And then, suddenly, out of nowhere, when I least expected it, the inevitable happened. The honeymoon was over. The let-down that can only be compared to that of January 2nd, when the holidays are over, and you're back to the mundane routine with a slightly fluffier mid-section and summer is the only thing to look forward to for months. Reality set in. And, by reality, I mean that lying bastard Satan and his tricky web of lies he weaves to keep you from fulfilling your purpose in life.

I had sat down at the computer. It was time to finally finish writing my book. It was time to re-launch the blog. It was time to launch the podcast. I had started writing this book approximately 13 months before, and the blog and podcast had been in the works for about six months. I stared at my computer. I looked at the words on the page written months before. "These are good," I thought. "The message is solid. It definitely comes from a place of purpose, takes ownership, shares wisdom, and empowers and reaches people. It actually sounds a lot like Rachel Hollis's message! Oh, that Rach, little does she know, we're going to be best friends one day and inspire women the world over to lead purpose-filled lives! It's so refreshing to see someone with your same view on life in this space… Uh! Oh No!"… My eyes widened, and breath suddenly caught in my throat. I felt my palms start to go sweaty, and the panic set in. The screeching sound of tires sliding to a stop rang through my mind, and I could envision myself locking down the brakes to avoid slamming into the back of the semi in front of me. I might as well have been the actor in that auto injury commercial where they call the tough, smart lawyer. That was the sound of my dreams coming to a screeching halt.

My mind raced as I processed all the thoughts. "Wait! Someone else has already done this. Someone else has already written the book I've dreamt of writing my entire life. Someone else has already created a movement for women everywhere to be inspired to live bigger lives, dream more, make an impact. Someone else has already, in the most brutally honest and lovingly compassionate way possible, told women to quit making their freaking excuses and live their best lives! Someone else has not only stepped into this space, but she *is* this space. There's not a woman I know that doesn't know about this book, rock a Made for More hat, watch her FB lives. She has a movie for goodness sakes! She's done it: Bigger, better, and most importantly, before me. Well, that's great! This is just about as good as that time I started doing yoga on the kid's swim mat in the lake as a means of multi-tasking while the kids played, only to find out "Boga" has since turned into the newest and greatest thing since sliced bread. I totally invented that. And, I totally had these words and this vision before she ever told me to wash my face. Oh yeah, and I was washing my face and telling others to do so first also. She beat me. While I had sat back thinking about finishing my book and launching my podcast, she had written my book. And, it had become a New York Times #1 Best Seller... Now what?" I kept watching, I kept listening, and I kept sharing. "It's not important who wrote the book anyway," I thought. "It's just important that the message is out there, and I will fully and completely support it in any way possible! But dang! Just think, if I would have gotten my book out first."

Fast forward a month or two. I quickly parked in a spot behind Ulta, the cosmetics store, hastily made my way into the Apple store and informed a store associate that my friend had called ahead to make me an appointment but that it was of utmost importance, and I needed to speak with someone about my phone as soon as possible. I'm fairly certain that I looked like a paranoid maniac. My heart was racing, breath rapid, and I kept looking over my shoulder until sweet Kasey showed up to take care of me. I handed him my shut off phone and explained—

"So, I work with some non-profit organizations mentoring survivors and speaking out against the bad guys. So, you know, there are people who might try and find some of the people I mentor... Anyway, my phone is doing totally crazy things. It looks like someone is remote accessing it and controlling it. I don't know if it's the Russian spies, traffickers, or a teenage cyber-criminal in his parent's garage, but someone has control of my phone & I'm freaking out." And then, after hysterically spewing all of the craziness out, I stood there, with all the composure and sanity one could muster in yoga pants, naked face, and dirty hair slapped under a ball cap.

Sweet Kasey: Okay, I get it. I understand. You work in some scary situations. You have every reason to be concerned, but let me at least put your mind to ease first. The likelihood of anyone hacking your phone is incredibly slim, and I believe your phone is ghosting. It's a common problem with the newest model, and I've seen it quite a bit. I'll run diagnostics and get you a new one in no time.

I breathed out a sigh of relief, instantly relaxed, and thanked Jesus.

Sweet Kasey: So, this work, with the people, and the bad guys... is it your business? Or is it volunteer work?

Me: Oh no, it's just something I'm really passionate about. It's all volunteer work.

Sweet Kasey: Cool, what about work? What do you do?

Me: I'm a business owner and have a few different businesses.

Sweet Kasey: What's your main one?

Me: "Well, my skincare business is the one that makes me money and supports the others.

Sweet Kasey: Cool. What are the others?

Me: Well, my husband and I are serial entrepreneurs with a few different businesses, but I'm working on a book, looking to re-launch my blog, and I'm starting a podcast.

Sweet Kasey: That's awesome! Give me the details. When does your podcast launch?

Me: Umm, September 6th.

Sweet Kasey: Is that a firm date? I want to tune in.

Me: Yeah, I mean, I think so. I've been working on this since January and just keep putting it off. I'm all ready to launch, but for some reason, I keep doubting myself and overanalyzing it. I mean, what am I going to say? What if I say something wrong? My voice is terrible. It's funny. I coach people every single day to seize the day, start now, start where they are, to do it scared, that fear is liar, that starting is the most important part of their journey. And, here I am, staring at a computer and microphone for months..."

Sweet Kasey: Just do it! Listen, someone out there needs to hear what you have to say. Can I ask you a question? Are you a believer?

Me: Yes, of course! That's a huge part of my platform.

Sweet Kasey: "Good! Don't shy away from that. Someone out there needs to hear what you have to say, and someone out there needs to hear Jesus in you.

I walked out of the store carrying my new, Russian spy-free phone to the car, breathing much easier, knowing I wasn't being watched or hacked and began processing the conversation. That's when I had the revelation. God gave me a voice for a reason. I have a story to share. Just because someone has gone before me doesn't mean I can't go. There is space at the table. God said the harvest is full, and he needs workers. And so, I went on to launch the podcast September 4th, 2018.

I fell in love with podcasting & enjoyed every minute of it. Editing is still totally weird for me, and I would much rather record the conversations and let someone else do the tedious tasks, but you do what you have to do in the beginning. I knew I needed to finish my book, but I just wasn't sure if that was the direction I was being called in at the time. However, every step of the way, someone would casually ask if I had a book out, or when I was going to write a book. I would post a descriptive narrative of our family vacation and get countless comments asking when I was going to write a book. A podcast listener would tell me how much they enjoyed the show and ask when I would have a book out. Each time, I would just smile and tell them I was working on it, when in all actuality, I hadn't sat down in front of my computer to write for months. Instead, I continued podcasting, speaking at any women's event I was invited to, and running my businesses.

One such event was a Women's Empowerment event I had accepted an invite to. I knew none of the organizers, speakers, or audience attendees, but I had committed to sharing my voice on whatever platform God called me to. The event was incredible, and the panel was full of powerful women following God's purpose for their lives. I mean, I was literally seated next to powerhouse influential Women of God. After the event, the organizer and I were chatting in that post-event high about how great it had been and all the possibilities for the future. We both felt like this could be something bigger, and we should lean into it. We decided to set up a meeting with the other speakers to discuss more events in the next year. Our organizer was a total go-getter and talking about a national tour with an event every quarter. I was so excited about the idea of that! It was exactly what I felt God calling me to do. I was fueled by pouring into women! However, after the initial meeting, I began to question if that was the life I really wanted. I had seen other major speakers in the arena lead an insanely busy schedule where they would be in a different city each night and spend more time in the air than on the ground. I had enough speaker friends to know that the life is not nearly as glamorous as it looks on Instagram. I started thinking about the sacrifices I would have to make, how many nights I would spend not sleeping in my own bed, the ridiculous amount of airplane germs I would be breathing in on the regular… In an effort to stay focused on one thing at a time, I quietly let that idea sink into the shadows and kept my head down working on the podcast while growing my business.

Tickets to the Rise conference went on sale in January. Rachel was going to be in Dallas, and I knew I had to go. I'll be honest; I didn't get tickets thinking this would change my life. In the spirit of full disclosure, I went into it thinking that I wouldn't hear anything I didn't already know, but it would be a great opportunity for networking. I mean, this audience would be full of my target audience, after all. As I settled in for the first day of the conference, I looked around at the 7,000 purpose-driven women in this audience. I breathed in the energy and excitement. I noticed how some ladies looked nervous, uncomfortable, and shy. I observed others exuding confidence and making friends with everyone. I settled into my seat, smiling to myself as I thought about how different we can all be but yet still possess the same internal yearning to fulfill our calling in life. The energy was absolutely electric as the conference center buzzed with women dancing and clapping along to the DJ, but it became explosive as the speakers took the stage.

As I listened to Rachel and the other speakers stand on stage, pouring their hearts and motivation into this crowd, the energy began to shift. I couldn't quite put my finger on it at first. It felt somewhat uncomfortable. I found myself distracted by this feeling and even a little agitated. It wasn't the energy of the room so much, but more my personal energy. I could feel my heart pounding so loudly I could hear it in my ears. I could feel my chest rising up and down with each breath that caught in my throat more rapid than the last. I could feel my palms sweating and could barely contain myself from jumping out of my seat. I could feel it rising up. Anger. It felt like anger. It was building and bubbling up to the surface until I felt like I would barely be able to contain it. I knew that I should be feeling incredibly empowered right now, but this was the opposite. I was pissed.

Being the self-aware female that I am, I leaned into what I was feeling and started unpacking it. What was making me angry at this conference? Why was I pissed? Was I jealous? What was this monster robbing me of the joy of a weekend of positivity, purpose, and empowerment? It wasn't the message being delivered; I totally agreed with what they were saying. I actually share a very similar message. It wasn't the speakers; they were my people: straight shooters, brutally honest, and on fire to inspire others to walk in purpose. It wasn't the platform, the environment, or the people around me. I sat there dumbfounded and questioning what the heck was going on here... until I realized. Me. It was me. It was the fact that I wasn't on that stage. I knew, in the very core of my soul, I was meant to be on that stage in this arena. Now, you may see this as jealousy. But my go-to emotion is anger. Not only is this my initial reaction to most things, but it's also the quickest way to get the most productivity out of me! Just ask my husband. The house is never cleaner than when I am too mad to even speak to him. And, well, Him being my creator and all, I'm pretty sure God knows that.

I realized I wasn't angry at any one person or situation, but I was angry because I hadn't answered God's call. I knew He had called me to write a book. I knew that He had called me to speak. I knew that He had given me a voice. And, instead of answering the call and sharing what he would have me share with the world, I was watching someone else do it. Somewhere around the exact moment that I was having this inner dialogue, Rachel asked a question, "Who here hasn't done what you feel called to do because you think someone else has already done it better than you?" People started raising their hands as she called on them, and they blurted out what it was. I was way up top in the cheap seats and knew there was no way she would hear my response, but I decided to yell it out anyway., "Like Rachel Hollis!" She stopped, turned immediately to face my section, and with the sincerest expression simply stated, "Sis, even Rachel Hollis wasn't Rachel Hollis until she was Rachel Hollis. You have to go do whatever it is that you're being called to do, and not worry about what someone else has done." Boom. I had a book that was 75% finished that had been sitting untouched because I was so afraid that I couldn't do it as well as someone else had. I had a platform that God had given me I hadn't stepped onto because I was afraid that I couldn't fill it as well as someone else could. God had given me everything I needed to do what he had called me to do, and I had disobediently declined the call. I looked down at the list of things that I wanted to accomplish and heard the words of my assistant in my ear "Bro, you need to finish your book already." I circled it. I would finish the book. And, I would also step onto any platform that God gave me from then on because it didn't matter who had gone before me, it just mattered I had been obedient and answered his call.

I've dug deep into what this particular phenomenon of the female psyche actually is. For me, It's not about jealousy, comparison, or even competition. I'm so dang proud and inspired when I see other women doing big things. It's something different. It's something that has been so deeply ingrained in us we don't even realize what it is when we feel it happening. For so long, we saw so few women who were leading. We saw so few with an opportunity to have a seat at the table. We subconsciously accepted the seats were limited, and if someone sat there first, then there could not be room for all of us. I've heard this referenced time and time again throughout my life, and I was actually cocky enough to think that I was far too confident of a female for this to ever affect me, until I too experienced the soul-crushing feeling of someone else fulfilling the purpose I had been called to. I didn't understand the feeling until I witnessed someone else shining their light as brightly as God had called me to shine mine. But what if? What if that whole "go and be a light unto the world" didn't look like one person shining one flashlight, but instead an entire army yielding spotlights?

In every arena we women step into, someone has to be first. Someone has to have stepped into it for us. It doesn't mean we can't join them there. It just means that they have paved the way for us to show up. Rachel had entered the space before me, but she did not fill the space. The response to her book just showed that women all over the world were HUNGRY for this. We were all struggling with the same battles each and every day but had chosen to not talk about them. In a world full of perfectly posted Instagram feeds, we needed more open, honest conversations like these.

When someone goes before us, it is a win for all of us. I don't believe that Ruth Bader Ginsburg was upset when Sandra Day O'Connor was appointed as the first-ever female Supreme Court Justice in 1981. Heck no man! I can imagine her right now, perched on the edge of her seat, watching Sandra swearing in on the television and fist-pumping the air. Althea Gibson had to be the first African American to play at Wimbledon so that Serena Williams could go on to be labeled one of the greatest, if not *the* greatest tennis players of all time. And when Kitty Wells belted out "It Wasn't God Who Made Honky Tonk Angels" at The Grand Ol' Opry, I bet she was beaming with pride at the thought of how many other daring women with a song in their heart and a refusal to not be silenced would one day stand on that stage. Each and every one of us gets to live in a day where we have not only a voice in our government, but also one where women are holding office and running for president thanks to the brave women who went before us and fought for that right. We must celebrate each other's victories but not let them lead us to shy away from our own.

This book, MY book, was my own. It was my story. No one could share the same words that God had given me to uniquely share. However, this story could only be shared if I obediently chose to step into the arena. So, to that note, I have to say thanks to all the women who have gone before me. Thank you for stepping into this arena: An arena in which there is more than enough room for as many Jesus-loving, business-hustling, brutally honest, wildly audacious women who want to take their seat at the table and show other women they have the power to accomplish anything they set their minds to.

How to Avoid the Comparison Trap:

1. Remind yourself that we are better together; collaboration over comparison.

2. Don't let someone else's success hold you back from your own calling in life.

3. Recognize that while we may be doing similar things, there is only one way that we can each serve our own unique purpose.

CHAPTER 11

Australia is Shady...

Remember when I said I started writing this book on a plane ride to Australia? It's time to share that part of the journey with you.

My husband and I made our way through the parking garage to our rental car. Having traveled for the past 24 hours, I hastily threw my bags in the backseat and couldn't wait to lay my head down at the hotel! I couldn't care less that it was 6 a.m. I just needed rest... and a shower. We smelled terrible. What is it about airplanes that make you feel so grimy?

I heard my husband at the front of the car say, "Umm.. babe. We have a problem. The steering wheel is on the wrong side of the car. How am I supposed to do this?" Delirious from the lack of sleep, we both burst out laughing. We knew we would be driving on the opposite side of the road, but for some reason, it never crossed our minds that the driver's seat would be opposite as well. Always one for an adventure, he jumped in, took the wheel, and told me we would figure it out. It's not really that different from the time we unloaded from a plane on a tiny island, took a cab to the marina, loaded our children along with all of our luggage onto a boat, which my husband had never driven, and then took it 22 nautical miles across an ocean he had never been on to an island we had never seen. It's always an adventure with this one. To say he pushes me to stretch outside of my comfort zone is putting it mildly. He and my children are scared of nothing, but I'm scared of everything.

He's convinced me to take helicopter rides that have required me to take a valium just in order to board. I've been drug through the Hawaiian rainforests suspended from a thin cable, over 250-foot-deep gulches with majestic waterfalls pouring into roaring rivers below... or so I'm told. My eyes were clenched shut so tightly for the duration of the two hours I'm fairly certain I can blame the need for eye cream on that nightmare. We've hiked through Central American rainforests filled with jaguars, monkeys, and the most poisonous snakes on Earth. None of which we saw, thanks to my ability to effectively produce enough noise to ensure no unwanted animals mistakenly stumbled across our path, never mind the fact we went with the intent of seeing jaguars. I narrowly survived a scuba adventure off the coast of Maui, where we were both tethered to one oxygen tank and had 20 feet of hose with which to descend to the depths of the sea. This was in the very early years of our relationship, and it most accurately foreshadowed the future years to come. He spent the entire time trying to pull me down deeper into the depths of the dark blue seas to observe the sea turtles, while I, hyperventilating, simultaneously swam furiously towards the surface. I've also sat in a small boat off the coast of Belize, watching in horror as my husband snorkeled in the midst of a shark feeding frenzy... with no guide, cage, or sense of protection...in seven foot of water. Thanks to the previous experience in Hawaii, we had already learned it was in everyone's best interest I stay on the boat. We've taken a brand new 38-foot motorhome pulling a 38-foot trailer without trailer brakes on a 3,000-mile road trip across roads and passes we've never crossed, including the Teton Pass. If you're not familiar with the winding road between Wyoming and Idaho, it's a high mountain pass filled with steep mountainous curves, hairpin corners, and 10% grades. In a motorhome. Pulling a trailer. With no trailer brakes. We were "fine"... or so he told me, as he always has, just like he did in all the other situations. We were always "fine." And embarking upon the Melbourne freeway running between the airport and St. Kilda, after traveling for 24 hours, was no different. We would, once again, be fine. This would be the first time for us to be away from our children for an extended period, and we were excited to have the time together.

We made our way down the freeway, on the other side of the car, on the other side of the road, on the other side of the world. We laughed every time he reached for the turn signal, and instead flipped the wipers on. Well, I laughed. He grumbled something along the lines of "Crap! Why does everything have to be backwards?" As we passed through Melbourne's CBD, a billboard out of the corner of my eye caught my attention. There were some words saying something about immigrants being targeted for Human Trafficking. "That's weird," I thought, "Australia has a problem with Human Trafficking... interesting." I don't typically pay attention to billboards. However, that particular one stood out. It seemed to be the only one of its kind in the area, and the bright colors and wording of the sign became ingrained in my mind. I couldn't look away.

I was there for the next few weeks for business. We had a busy agenda ahead of us filled with meetings and trainings to help launch my Australian team. The first night in Melbourne, our sleep schedules were so jacked up my husband decided to go to sleep at 5 p.m., and I decided to make my way down to the restaurant in the lobby to do some work. Armed with my laptop, I grabbed a seat at the bar, leaving two seats between a couple and me. The couple talked loudly, laughed incessantly, and eventually invited me into the conversation. They were intrigued by the American with the Texan accent and immediately wanted to know my thoughts on our current president and gun control. They were shocked I could have such a diplomatic conversation while they poked and prodded. As the conversation and night wound down, they let me know they had really enjoyed our conversation, thought I was absolutely delightful, and wondered if I would like to do some coke in the bathroom with them. I thanked them for the invite but let them know the glass of red wine in front of me was my only drug of choice. And then, flattered as I was, I took my laptop, made my way back to the room, and woke my husband up to let him know I had been offered coke. He muttered something about Dr. Pepper and rolled over to continue his snoring serenade.

The next few days in Melbourne were filled with nonstop activity, and we were taking it all in. We were able to spend some time with our good friends, do some sight-seeing and enjoy a burger at their restaurant. My favorite part about the internet is the ability to stay in touch with friends from all over the world so that when you do visit their country, they can show you around, and you don't feel like such a tourist. While we were in Melbourne, we headed to the country (or Bush), to visit my team members. The intention was to host training and launch events, but what we hadn't expected was that we were also invited into their lives. We were welcomed in with open arms to meet their families, share dinner with them, see some kangaroos, and take a riverboat cruise. As we forged relationships, I found myself having conversations in which my beliefs and "talk of God" were brought up as something unusual for my new friends. Although my faith was uncommon, I realized that life in the Bush of Australia doesn't look much different than country life in Texas. Our time in Melbourne was over too soon, and we headed up to Brisbane for a few days. We made our way back to the airport with much more ease than we had first embarked upon the same highway at arrival and scooted through security with only one minor glitch. Somewhere between security and the restroom, I passed a poster hanging on the wall about shoulder level. There was a picture of a young girl on it and something mentioning missing children and human trafficking. "How weird! There's something else about human trafficking. And this time it is referencing children being trafficked rather than immigrants. This must really be an issue over here," I thought as I made my way into the bathroom stall. I couldn't recall any time that I had ever even read the words "human trafficking" in America, more or less seen billboards and posters bringing awareness to it.

We boarded the plane and landed in Brisbane two hours later. I immediately fell in love with the beautiful city. The sun was shining for what seemed like the first time since we had been in Australia. It had been dark and dreary while we were in Melbourne, which was to be expected, considering it was the end of autumn. We landed at a nice little hotel nestled in the center of Kangaroo Point, which was quite possibly the cutest little neighborhood I had ever seen. We could walk to a cute pub, enjoy Asian food next door, round the corner to the coffee shop, or stop in the market one street over. We could access any stop in the city by taking a short walk down to the ferry stop and boarding a water taxi or ferry. We did just that one evening as we took the hotel manager's restaurant recommendation and headed out for dinner. The breeze was cool, and we enjoyed the ride as we watched lights from the buildings dancing across the water underneath Story bridge. That meal consisted of quite possibly the best seafood we have ever had. The entire evening was blissfully idyllic. Brisbane was less rushed with only one business meeting, so we were really able to enjoy the city. It was dreamy and romantic and felt like we were on more of a vacation than a business trip. After arriving back at the hotel, we spent some time on the patio visiting with the hotel manager and other guests. The manager and I had a long conversation that evening where he questioned me about God, mental health, and suicide. He shared with me his personal battle with depression, anxiety, and questioning whether God loved him. I truly believe that these instances in which we allow people to ask the hard questions and come from a place of love and mercy, allow us to enter into kingdom conversations. These intimate settings are often-times far more significant than any message you can share from a stage.

We left Brisbane and headed to the Gold Coast, and we were so excited about this leg of the trip. We would drive the coastline down to Sydney, stopping a couple of nights along the way. It was a peaceful drive with lush foliage creating a canopy over the road and breath-taking sea-scape views scattered with signs warning of Koala crossings. Much to my dismay, I didn't spot a Koala in a tree, but it wasn't for lack of effort. Our first night's stay was in Byron Bay, which is a common vacation spot for Aussies. One way in, one way out, and way too many people for my husband's preference. I personally loved it! It was a neat little, artistic town with street performers on the sidewalks and barefoot, dread-clad hippies roaming the streets with their leash-less dogs. As we strolled down the sidewalk past music drifting from acoustic instruments and aromas from a nearby crêpery wafting through the air, one young lady caught my eye. She looked similar to that of the other gypsy-like individuals, but there was something else that stopped me in my tracks. Her appearance was disheveled, and her eyes glazed over in a manner that indicated she was under the influence of something. But, through the frizzy brown hair that clung to her face, I could see a sadness. Her eyes, although glazed over, seemed to be searching. As her gaze darted around the streets, it eventually landed on me. We stood there, across the street from one another, eyes locked, and no words uttered. But, I could feel her desperate cry for help. I didn't know what she needed, but her sadness was heavy. The moment was interrupted as one of the men with her grabbed her by the arm and led her down the sidewalk. She glanced back over her shoulder at me as she and the two men walked away with stray dogs trailing. I couldn't shake the cold chill that her sorrowful stare had sent down my spine. I took a deep breath, pulled my jacket tighter, and we headed back to the room. We packed up the next morning, leaving Byron Bay and the sad girl in the rearview as we continued our journey.

Sydney was our final destination on our trek across Oz. We would spend a few days there, meet up with some more team members, and then eventually board a plane to head back home to our kids. We never spent more than two nights in one place for the entire trip and didn't make reservations made ahead of time. We would get there, drive around neighborhoods, check out some spots I had looked up, and then eventually make a decision. Once in Sydney, we made our way to a suburb where I had found a hotel. As we drove down the street, looking at the neighborhood, it suddenly felt grimy. I saw a neon sign that just read 'GIRLS'. My husband quickly exclaimed, "That chick is wearing lingerie." It was mid-afternoon, so you can imagine our surprise. There were several people, men and women, parading around, half-dressed, with cigarettes dangling from their lips in the sunlight. The entire neighborhood had a feeling of heroin and debauchery. It was heavy, and I didn't like it. Between the human trafficking signs and posters, the sad girl in Byron Bay, and now this, I was suddenly ready to be back home where everything felt much safer. We quickly decided it was not the neighborhood for us and instead headed to Darling Harbour, where we found the most delightful boutique hotel for the last few days of our trip.

If you've never been to Sydney, I highly recommend this neighborhood. The food, shops, seafood market, and local attractions are incredible. We took time out to enjoy a date night on a dinner cruise where we gazed upon the Sydney Opera House and the Sydney Harbour

Bridge. The time eventually came to head to the airport and go home to see our babies! As we hurriedly rolled our suitcases through the airport, I was pulled to the side for a more in-depth security check. While I was awaiting my pat-down, my eyes nervously roamed around the holding room where they landed on, once again, a poster about missing children being trafficked. What on earth was up with Australia and this trafficking issue? I would definitely need to research this problem when I was back in the states. I was eventually released from the tiny room with glass walls and a very unfriendly security officer, to board a plane, make the excruciating 17 hour flight back home, re-live the same day twice as we crossed time zones, and eventually land on the sweet soil of Texas ground. But somehow, I had this feeling that my life was changed from that trip. I felt in my soul that this trip served a greater part of my story than just the global expansion of my skincare business. It felt like a journey.

In the mundane routine of our day to day lives, it can be difficult for us to truly hear (not audibly) clear direction from God. When we find ourselves seeing the same people, going to the same places, and doing the same activities day in and day out, it is often easy to not look outside the bubble of familiarity and comfort. We don't take time to notice the detail of our surroundings. We don't stop to have the deep conversations. And, we don't pause to truly see the people around us. You see, nothing that I observed in Australia was any different than what was happening at home. It just so happens that because I was out of my comfort zone, I was acutely aware of my surroundings and the people within them.

Ways To Seek Direction Outside Of Your Comfort Zone

1. Step out of your routine and go somewhere unknown: A new coffee shop, a trip out of town, or a trip out of the country.

2. Speak to people you don't know. Take a genuine interest in their story and hear them.

3. Pay attention to your surroundings. How are they different than your own? How are they similar?

4. See people. Truly stop to observe their actions, body language, and nature. See them as humans.

5. Take the opportunity to be quiet and listen without the day to day interruptions.

CHAPTER 12

Serve Where You Are

You know how, when you get a brand new shiny white SUV, you start to see shiny white SUVs everywhere you look? Like, once you see it, you just can't unsee it? After getting home from Australia, and the jet lag wore off, I started seeing the topic of human trafficking pop up everywhere! All of a sudden it was in my social media feed. It was on the local news channels. I was seeing billboards. I instantly realized it must be a problem in more countries than just Australia, and I had to do something about it! I mean, I had to help those other people in those other countries! I had gone to school for International Studies and focused on issues with women and children, so this might even be my higher calling. Up until then, I had thought 2017 would be the year that I would take a mission trip to Africa and adopt an orphan, but maybe this was it. I started researching and reading about human trafficking. I sought out organizations that were fighting human trafficking, and while on my search, I realized that this was not solely a problem in Australia. This was not a problem only occurring in developing countries. This was not merely a problem for immigrants. This was a growing epidemic happening in our backyards. I wanted absolutely nothing to do with it. When the idea was that it was an international problem I could get involved in fighting, it was okay. But, when it came down to being American girls and looking completely different than the movie, *Taken*, I wanted no part. I became incredibly fearful and wasn't sure that God knew what he was doing putting this cause on my heart. I mean, adopting orphans from Africa just seemed so much more sparkly to me. However, this call would not let go of me. I began pouring over articles online, and in such research, found an organization called A21 and immediately recognized the bright graphics from something I had seen in Australia. I poured over the statistics, stories, survivor reports, and knew immediately if I was going to be involved, this was the organization for me. They were young, socially savvy, proactive, grassroots abolitionists. They were everything I had admired about the Peace Corp with a whole lot of Jesus behind them!

Armed with new facts, I shared some of this epidemic I had learned about in Australia with my dad and stepmom. They quickly told me the guy who had bought our house while we were in Australia was involved with fighting child trafficking. He had some type of organiztion, where he helped kids, and he had shared with them how the local casino was a hotbed for trafficking. This blew my mind! We had never met the people who had bought our house because the closing date happened while we were in Australia. Since my stepmom was the realtor, they had done all of the leg work for us. How crazy was it that the buyer was involved in the same cause I was researching? Up until then, I didn't know a single person who was concerned with this cause, more or less fighting it.

I started talking with a few friends of mine about my recent discoveries. These girls had started out as a group of accountability partners in my business but had evolved into more of the type of people that push you to be the best version of yourself in all areas of life. I shared with them that this cause was heavy on my heart, and I thought God was calling me to it. They of course, encouraged me to pursue it. That fall, our church ladies' group was attending a Propel Women's Conference. I had no idea who Christine Caine was, but I was excited for the conference, so I started digging in. I realized she was the founder of A21, so this must mean I was meant to attend this conference and be involved with this organization. Just two weeks after registering for the conference, one of my accountability girlfriends sent a video by Christine Caine to the group. It was a motivational video about being called to your purpose. I instantly thought, "Wow! This lady just won't leave me alone. She's chased me from Australia, to my ladies' church group, and now into my accountability group as well." I asked my girlfriend if she knew that Christine was the founder of A21 and the Propel conference I was going to. Her exact words, "No, but if that's not a push from God, I don't know what the hell is. When are you going to finally realize that you're not running anything and relinquish control?" I explained it was a matter of fear. This was a dark and heavy issue that I wasn't sure I wanted to open myself up to. In my mind, I envisioned traffickers coming after me. Being a businesswoman, I know I don't appreciate anyone messing with my money, so I assumed the same went for the bad guys. I had young children and didn't want to put them at risk. I was scared. Plain and simple. I will never forget her words ringing in my ears that day. "If you're scared to even get involved with the fight against it, how scared do you think that girl is that is currently trapped in slavery?" I instantly could see a young girl all alone in a cold room, a shell of herself, with eyes only filled with fear and pain. I knew that I had to help her… I just had no idea how. So, I started praying and researching. There had to be some way I could answer the call God had put on my heart.

Do you ever find yourself wide awake in the middle of the night, unable to let your mind rest and fall asleep? You wake up suddenly as if someone shook you awake and think, "Oh my gosh! I have to do something!' But you don't know what. I'm not certain if it was my mom or grandma, but someone told me at a young age that this was God waking us up for a reason, and we should use the time to pray. That's what I normally do. And, being the neurotic, worst-case scenario nut job that I am, I typically think it means I need to pray fervently for every single family member and friend that might not wake up in the morning. See? Neurotic. However, this time it was different. I was awake, staring at the ceiling, heart pounding, breath caught in my throat, and I knew there was a reason I was awake. It was 3:00 in the morning. My eyes had literally jolted open as if someone had called my name while shaking me violently. My breathing was rapid, and I laid there, gathering my thoughts. This whole human trafficking and A21 thing kept bouncing around inside my head like a pinball machine. I closed my eyes tightly, tried to calm my breath, and started praying. "Yes Lord. Yes. I'm here. Use me. Where you go, I'll go. Lead me and I will follow. Amen. Goodnight." One rapid breath… young girl all alone in a room…two rapid breaths…Christine Caine's video…three rapid breaths…billboard in Melbourne…four rapid breaths…*move your feet*…five rapid breaths… *Serve where you are.*

These last two statements I heard played through my mind no less than 24 times in the next two hours. At 5:00 in the morning, I gave up on sleep and went to my office. I pulled out my Jesus Calling devotional in order to try to get some type of answer to this call keeping me awake. Thinking I was turning to the scripture cited for that morning's devotional, I turned to Matthew 10:27, "What I tell you in the darkness, speak in the light; what is whispered in your ear, proclaim from the housetops." I thought that was spot on. He had been speaking to me all night. I sat there staring at my computer thinking about what I had wrestled with all night long and my newfound God nudge to speak the truth in the light and proclaim it from the housetops. But what was *it*? What was I meant to share? I thought back to the resounding statements: "Move your feet. Serve where you are." I remembered there was an upcoming Walk for Freedom with A21 that I could be a part of and thought that would work since I would be moving my feet. I read the instructions for hosting a walk carefully and realized this was the literal first step to fulfilling this calling. But I needed to speak it in the light. So, I decided rather than wake anyone up at an ungodly time of the morning, I would reach for email, and with rapid breaths, pounding heart, and shaky hands, I furiously typed out an email asking my pastors if they'd be willing to get involved in the fight against human trafficking.

From there, my pastor's wife and I scheduled a sit down to discuss this further. I shared with her this calling I was feeling more in-depth, and how I needed some type of validation to let me know this was from God, and not something I was doing "for me." I had this fear people would somehow misunderstand my intentions and feel it was more of a do-good, look at me type of involvement rather than an act of faith. Her response is what I revert to anytime I feel the enemy attacking: "One of the best ways to know that something is from God is to ask yourself if this is anything you would have ever been involved with by your own choosing. If not, you know it's from God, and you follow it. And then, well, listen, haters gonna hate!" We spent the rest of our time together planning out the Walk for Freedom and strategizing about community involvement. She told me she was happy to stand by my side and walk next to me through this. Looking back, I'm amazed she said yes so quickly. Having gotten to know her better in the last couple of years, I know planning things on such a large scale freaks her out. She's a super detailed person and wants every last-minute detail planned before saying yes. Me, on the other hand, with top strengths being Achiever and Activator, I have an idea and put it into action while working the details out later. I like to think that God placed me in her life to make her a little more spontaneous and her in mine to make me more detail-oriented.

Armed with my "go forth" pastoral approval and fervent zeal for this newly called purpose, I began planning. I put a call in to the human trafficking specialist at the local crisis center and was so excited when she called me back. I spilled out my idea of hosting the local Walk for Freedom and asked if she and the center would like to partner up for this. She very quickly, and much to my dismay, said no. She very quickly shared how A21 was a global organization, and if we brought attention to human trafficking in that manner, people would think it was a global problem and not happening here locally. I felt the wind rush out of my sails. Since I had started this whole proclaiming thing, she was the first to tell me no. I listened to her excuses and decided to schedule an in-person meeting with her to discusses it more in-depth.

My friend and I headed over to the meeting with excitement and nerves to hear more about what we could do to fight it in our country. I was fully prepared to plead my case as to why this organization should get on board with us. As we sat in the room with the two women, we learned facts, stories, and data about this growing epidemic. They explained how people don't want to believe it's happening all around them, so they didn't want to bring attention to it at the global level, only at a local level. I kept feeling a tug on my heart that I didn't need to let them talk me out of this. I can remain undaunted when someone tells me I can't, but I tend to let it add fuel to the fire. I shared with the ladies all of the ways A21 was serving at both a local and global level and explained why I thought they should reconsider. One of them responded with a furrowed brow and pursed lips, and in an over-enunciated slowly spaced manner, "Well, Christine Caine is an *international speaker.*" I sat across the desk, looking at her and realized this was the exact limited mindset that frustrated me. Who taught this lady to play small? She was doing big things! God's work kind of things! She was serving widows and orphans, being the hands and feet of Jesus. Why did she think those hands only reached this county? I realized she wasn't coming on board with my mission but decided I could learn all I could about human trafficking at a local level from her. She convinced me I needed to become a certified advocate with this organization in order to gain access to a human trafficking coalition.

As I sat through the two weeks of daily classes, I found the information not only shocking but almost more than I could handle. I remember my husband waking me up in the middle of the night to ask if I was okay because I was crying in my sleep. I remember waking up from nightmares unable to go back to sleep, with the scenarios playing over and over in my mind. I remember lying awake one night thinking I wanted nothing to do with any of this and eventually sternly saying to God, "Okay God, if you've called me to this. If you want me to fight for these victims, I need something from you. I have to be able to sleep at night. You must give me rest without my mind racing thinking about all the evils of the world." And then, God granted my request.

I'll never forget August 31st of that year. It had been a very crucial month for my skincare business. I had a huge goal to hit, and it was going to take all hands on deck from my team. In all honesty, I should have been focused on this goal the entire month, but I was busy doing God's work and had let my business slide. As I left the four-hour advocacy training that evening with an incredibly heavy heart from what we had just been taught, I checked my back office. The numbers were not there. My team was not going to make it, and it seemed as if none of them cared. Surely God had not brought me this business and this calling for either of them to suffer. Surely, He wanted me to continue to walk in abundance and be able to bless others. Surely, He didn't want me to turn my back on the hundreds of women on my team that counted on me. How on earth would I balance this business and this calling?

How could I do both?. I was mentally and emotionally exhausted. I felt like a lone ship at sea that could not see any other vessel, person, or coastline in sight. I sobbed the entire 25-minute drive home. I cried out to God, cried out. I did not whisper; I did not mumble. I went boldly before the throne of God. I cried out, "God! If you want this mountain moved, you *have* to send me the people. I cannot do this alone." I knew He had plans for me: plans to prosper me and not to harm me, plans of hope and a future. And, He did. I just had to wait for His timing.

As I awaited the first Coalition meeting, I spent countless hours scrolling their social media pages researching the various organizations involved. While I knew my advocacy training at the crisis center was part of the journey, I knew it was not where God was calling me. I knew I was not being called to front line ministry. I felt all along that I was called to serve survivors from a place of overcoming and help them be restored. I wasn't called to rescue victims. I was called to speak to warriors. I had relinquished the idea of hosting the local walk, and in turn, had registered a team for a walk further away. I decided I could attend the walk and learn how to host one of my own in the future. While I knew that A21 was where my heart was called, I also knew I needed to be involved at a local level. Day in and day out, I combed through websites and mission statements of organizations searching for how I could "Serve Where I Was". I found one organization that was an aftercare home for sexually exploited and trafficked survivors. These women were all over the age of 18, and I found this interesting because they were amongst the minority of those I saw being advocated for. Most of the organizations I was finding were all geared for children. While I did feel this was a crucial outreach, I also felt the women of age needed an advocate. They needed restoration. I signed up for an open training call they posted online, and within ten minutes of being in the meeting, I knew this organization was one I was called to. At the end of the training, I went up to the city and house directors and shared how I had a heart for these women. I told them my strengths were public speaking and mentoring, and they could use me however they needed. We left the meeting, and my friend asked me what I thought. I told her this was exactly where God needed me at the local level. I said it would be awesome if the church ladies could take the aftercare home residents to the Propel Conference with us. Her eyes grew wide, panic set in, and she started telling me how there wasn't enough time to plan it. I sent the directors an email the very next day, telling them all the ways I would be willing to serve. I contacted people with Propel in order to secure discounted tickets for the women and staff. I awaited approval from the organization… and I waited…and I waited. I finally received an answer from the City Director informing me the residents would be unable to attend the conference but that my "patience with her was outstanding!' I literally laughed out loud and responded it had nothing to do with patience, but persistence, I was nothing if not persistent.

Shortly after, she emailed, asking if I could teach a 12-week class over boundaries to the residents. I prayed about it for about 2 minutes and immediately responded with yes. I had no idea what to expect within the house, but knew that this was where God had called me to serve. I knew that I had a heart for inspiring and empowering survivors.

I came to the house one Wednesday afternoon excited and anxious to be meeting two new girls I would begin a weekly class with. I sat down in the living room, ready to get to know these ladies. She sat there silently, drawing in her binder and not looking up. I finally asked her to tell me what she thought about the book, as well as the upcoming class. Her response was, "I ain't ever had no boundaries, nobody never taught me no boundaries, and I don't need to read a book about boundaries." I nodded my head, taken aback a bit as this was my first one on ones with the girls.

"Well, it's an assigned class, and you have to do it, so I guess we'll just get through it together," I told her. The following week, I returned to teach the class, and after just two chapters, had a completely different student sitting before me.

As I walked in, she excitedly told me, "Miss Brandi, I love this book! It's changed my life. I wish I would have had it fifteen years ago!" She carried that excitement throughout the rest of the book!

We had one lady in the house that I met the first night I was invited over for dinner. She had just arrived to the program. The first time I met her was when I took dinner to the house. She was quiet and withdrawn but joined us at the table. She kept her head and eyes down and only glanced up occasionally when someone asked her a question or passed a dish. After finishing her meal, clearing her plate, and thanking me for dinner, she excused herself to her bedroom for the rest of the evening. I gave her space and didn't push. My only hope was she could eventually see Jesus in me and feel loved, welcome, and safe. She continued to be very withdrawn and standoffish. It took months for me to get her to speak to me. Each time I came in, I would say hi to her, and she would obligingly respond as her eyes shifted away from me. I could feel her pain, doubt, and lack of confidence in humanity.

On Valentine's Day, I decided to do something special for the girls. I took them each a bouquet of flowers, a necklace, and a card with a scripture unique to them. As she saw the flowers, I watched her eyes start to light up. Then, as she read, I witnessed her face soften, a smile began to spread across her lips, and her eyes tear up. She looked up at me through those sparkling teary eyes, "Aw! No one's ever got me flowers." I received a card the next day from the girls thanking me. Her line specifically read, "Thank you for everything. You make me feel like you actually care about us." And just like that, she knew I cared. Over the course of the next few months, I was able to see her blossom like a flower. Each week, she became a little more open. And then one day, when I showed up, she was sitting outside in the sun, looking radiant and smiling ear to ear. She hugged me and told me all about her new job and how great everything was going. I not only watched her graduate but also have witnessed her flourish in life.

It was time for the annual celebration dinner, and I had secured a donor that contributed money towards a shopping trip for the girls to get new outfits for the banquet. As we loaded up to go shopping, Ms. "I ain't got no boundaries" asked if she could ride in my new Jeep. She had been asking for a ride ever since I first pulled up in it. She happily hopped in with me as we made our way to the department store. With a huge grin and a sparkle in her eyes, she said, "Ms. Brandi, I have to tell you all about this weekend!" The absolute joy radiating from her eyes at that moment is something I will never forget! The girls had attended a retreat over the weekend, and she wanted to tell me all about it! "Remember how I was nervous about being around those church people with my tattoos and if they would judge me? Well, the first night at dinner, they gave us a rose!" she exclaimed while she pointed to the rose tattoo on her left hand. "And, the second night, they gave us a necklace with this on it!" she pointed to the crown tattoo on her right hand. "And, the third night, they had us write down everything bad we've ever done and everything bad that ever happened to us. Then, they had us go up and put it all on this big wooden cross. And then… They burned it! Ms. Brandi! You know how I always thought I had to have a man to be happy? Well, I don't no more. I fell in love with Jesus, and he's all I need!" When I tell you that I had goosebumps in that Jeep and could feel Jesus's love, grace, and mercy beaming down, there is no way I can fully describe that feeling. I get goosebumps now just talking about it!

As I spent more time in the house, I began to not only build relationships with the ladies but also understand childhood trauma on a deeper level. I was able to see my mother in some of the women. I was able to see how a childhood without boundaries carries over into adulthood. Each week I was humbled by the women's determination, and each week, I was moved by God's transformation in their lives.

How to Unlock Your Purpose:

1. Be obedient to God's call. Say yes, over and over again, even when you don't know what you're saying yes to.

2. Have a servant's heart. Put your ego aside and decide to serve others however they need you to.

3. Be persistent. Your purpose will not arrive at your door ready for you to unwrap it. You must persistently pursue it.

CHAPTER 13

Smiling Through the Rain

Our Labor Day looked different than what it ordinarily would have. On the surface, it looked pretty similar. We planned for some off-roading, took the jet ski out, went out on the boat, tubed, and cooked out. The ribs were a perfect combination of juicy, tender meat falling off the bone and a crispy bark-like outer layer. The jalapeño and cream cheese stuffed pork tenderloin with its intricately woven bacon basket was a culinary delight! And, the traditional sides of pasta salad, crunchy coleslaw, and spicy beans scattered the table. The tables and chairs were arranged, and we eagerly awaited our guests' arrival. We had special guests coming who hadn't been out before, so everything had to be just right. And then, just as we were launching the jet ski in preparation for the ladies I mentor, the skies clouded up, and rain began falling. This couldn't be happening. God and I had talked this through. I just needed him to hold the rain off for a few hours. I would need it to clear up.

Our guests arrived and thankfully the rain had made its exit. We made quick introductions, hopped on the ranger, and took a ride around the lake. There were evens of us and not enough seat belts, but we crammed in with reckless abandonment and wild giggles. After a quick tour, it was time to eat. It was a feast fit for a king, and we were glad the weather and family emergencies had provided for a low guest attendance in order for us to have plenty of leftovers. We quickly cleaned up the meal and headed down the hill to put the boat in.

The girls climbed into the boat, so excited to be on the lake. Some of the girls were from rural areas, so they appreciated the nature aspect of the hills, trees, and water. One girl kept telling me how much it reminded her of home and how happy her soul felt out here. I agreed. There's just something about the serenity of the lake that soothes the soul and heals the heart.

We took off across the lake just in time to see the skies once again cloud up and water start raining down. Typically, my husband would have no part of having a boat out in the rain. But the girls looked at the sky and back at me. "We're not going in, are we? It's okay. We don't mind getting wet." He knew the girls wanted a day on the boat. We turned and tried outrunning the rain, but it kept coming. The rain stung our faces, and we had to squint to see, as we huddled under the cover of the boat, towels held over our heads, making our way speedily back to the dock for a break. However, the three girls in the front of the boat were unscathed. They kept smiling ear to ear, laughing, and telling me they didn't care if it was raining, they were having a blast!

As we pulled up to the dock, the rain was letting up, and my kid was riding around the cove on the jet ski. And it just so happened I had five girls who were eager for a jet ski ride. He, being the sweet kid he is, kindly obliged. We all shared belly laughs while watching first-timers try to learn how to load up on a jet ski without falling off and taking the driver with them. Trying his best to give them an action-packed ride without throwing them off, he only dumped a couple. They later told me he's a strong little guy because they were holding on to him for dear life, and he never let go of the handlebars.

With the jet ski tours out of the way it, was tubing time. I was surprised that two of the girls were so eager to jump on a tube with it being their first time, but they were ready! Of course, we did have to overcome a few hesitations about alligators and Lochness monsters, but we assured them that in our decades of spending time on this lake, we had yet to be eaten. As we hammered down on the throttle and pulled the two away from the dock, each on their own tubes, their eyes got big, mouths dropped open, and shrieks of delight (mixed with a slight touch of terror) could be heard over the roar of the boat motor. We pulled them in circles and snake-like patterns all over the lake for quite some time, until we saw the end of the ride result in one being flung off the tube and into the water. They all came up smiling and made their way back to the boat to allow the others to have a turn.

The next two climbed on top of their tubes and prepared for the ride ahead. It didn't take long before we lost one. She came up hysterically laughing to report that it was lake, one, and her, zero. The last ride was epic. We twisted, turned, circled, and slung each of them in and out of the wake. At one point, I wasn't sure if the girls were laughing or crying. The last and final corner we took sent the same girl once again hurling through the air and completing an impressive series of barrel rolls across the top of the water, until she was slung off yelling, "That was fun!"

The skies were getting dark again, and it was closing in on the time our friends would have to leave to get back to their house in time. The first two ladies wanted one more, quick ride before they had to say goodbye. As they were attempting to climb back onto the tubes, the skies parted, and the rain came down! As we all made our rain-soaked way back to the house for towels and dry clothes, it was time for goodbyes. They all hugged and thanked us for having us out, but what they didn't realize was just how much of a blessing it was having them. In the words of my husband, "The smiles on those girls' faces made everything worth it!"

While volunteering in the house, I quickly found that while rewarding, it was emotionally draining work. I'll never forget when it felt like the literal rug had been pulled from beneath my feet, and I had to question God as to why on earth he would ask me to be involved with such a cycle of dysfunction. We had one girl in the house I had made an immediate connection with. She had a radiant spirit, brilliant mind, and despite the struggles in her life, she still possessed the ability to dream big. I knew God had a plan for her to share her testimony with the world. Every time I saw her, I would speak life into her, and she would receive it. She believed in herself and desired to help other women do the same. I lived for her giant, full-body, embracing hugs each time I arrived. And then, one day, I showed up, and she didn't come to welcome me. I visited with the other girls for a bit, and finally, realizing she wasn't around, asked where she was.

"She gone," one girl told me. I looked on with confusion and searched the other faces to see if I could make some sort of sense out of the situation. One looked down with sadness on her face. Another voice chimed in with a "yeah, she bounced." And, that was it. As a volunteer, you're not allotted all the details of situations, so to this day; I'm not sure exactly what happened. I know this was the first moment I realized they weren't all going to complete the program. This was her second time in the program. She was so incredibly grateful for the opportunity, and the fact she didn't complete it looked to me like the devil had won. Up until then, I had ignorantly thought every girl who came through the door would automatically stay in the program. In my mind, with the horrendous circumstances they had been through before the house, they would be eternally grateful for this team, this opportunity, a warm bed to sleep in, and a roof over their heads. It had never ever crossed my mind they would just leave. A few short weeks later, another girl was gone when I showed up. When she came into the program, she shared with me that she had spent two nights out of an entire year sleeping under a roof. And now, she was back out there. Somewhere, most likely, not under a roof. Not supported with a staff of trained professionals. Not being poured into and loved on in a safe environment where she can be fully restored.

I found myself struggling to keep going. I felt burnout setting in. I felt hopelessness. I had just been fighting this fight for less than a year; it had already become too hard. I was overwhelmed with the inability to help them. I'm a fixer by nature, so it's quite interesting God would place me in one of the most unfixable positions possible. I found myself asking God if it was all really worth it. Was the work that he was asking me to do worth it? How could I be following his will and purpose if these people kept turning from Him? How could he be leading me away from my kids, husband, and my business to do work that was fruitless? How was this truly His plan? I felt helpless and empty. It is one thing to hear of people struggling in life, but it is an entirely different thing to see them come so close to healing only to fall back, leaving you wondering if even God can pull them out of the insane state of Hell that they're living in. It is simply the crazy cycle that is a direct result of their trauma. I don't have a license in this department. But I have firsthand witnessed the aftermath, and it sure is a difficult situation for those of us trying to speak life into it.

I remember spending countless hours on the phone with one of my mentors, pouring my heart into him about these situations. At some point in the conversation, I remember saying, "What are we doing here? I mean, if they just keep going back to the same destructive cycle and refuse the help, aren't we just wasting our time trying to help them?"

I can hear his baritone raspy voice now as he first paused to take a long drag of his cigarette and exhaled the smoke with a long sigh. "Listen," he said, "it's not your job to save them. You are placed in their lives at a specific time, and it's your job to put some God in them. You are there for a reason, to speak life into them and left them know that they are loved, valued, and worthy. And then, regardless of whether they are a success statistic or not, you know that no matter where they end up at in life, they can remember that you told them Jesus loved them, and you loved on them. That's it. That's all you can do." That's it. That's all I or anyone else can do. It's not up to us to save them. It's up to us to love them. And, for my own personal wellbeing, I have to cling to the good times when I find myself searching for meaning in the hopeless place. When I learn one of the residents left the program and ended up back in jail, I think back to her riding a tube behind the boat, in the midst of the pouring rain, grinning from ear to ear and laughing with the sheer joy of a young child. When I hear that one of the graduates has fallen back into old habits with the old crowd, I have to remember her standing at graduation, hands stretched to the sky, tears streaming down her face, praising the one who created her. And I know, in that moment, that we showed them Jesus. I'm reminded of God's grace for us. All I can think is that we, God's children, disappoint Him every day. We make poor decisions and leave Him disappointed. But, we persevere and know that above all, He is God. He is mercy, grace, and love.

I think back to the girls on the tube that day on the lake. They had been through Hell and back in their lives. They had been sexually exploited, homeless, addicted to drugs, and experienced things I can't even wrap my mind around. They were thousands of miles away from friends and family, living in a houseful of complete strangers. They formed a community and were loved and supported by new friends like us and many others. But more than that, they were a blessing to our lives by showing us we could smile through the rain, ride out the storm, and be grateful for each new experience!

One of the most impactful lessons I've learned as a privileged individual is this: when our lives are going well, it is easy to shy away from God. We tend to think we can handle whatever situation comes our way on our own. When we experience great success, we can start to think we achieved it on our own and not remember who helped us get there. However, when we find ourselves in dire situations with no choice other than to depend on God, we lean on Him. This is what he desires. And so, we have to make the cognizant decision to place ourselves in close proximity with those who have no choice but to be dependent upon Him in efforts to keep us focused on our true Redeemer.

CHAPTER 14

The Weird Space

C
ruising down the highway in our gorgeous new rig, we were
headed back from a 2,800-mile, eight-state road trip with my
family. I sat in the passenger seat, scrolling through Facebook. It
had been an incredible vacation. We had camped in remote locations,
experienced beautiful scenery, covered stretches of treacherous
highway, had the thrill of extreme off-roading, relished quality family
time, explored historical landmarks, and met some of the friendliest
new people along the way. It was an amazing ten days full of memories
to last a lifetime. As we were nearing home, I began going over a mental
checklist for the upcoming 4th of July weekend at the lake. I went over
the list out loud with my husband, the things that needed to be done
the next day: boat maintenance, grocery supplies, lawn maintenance,
church camp supplies, and the list went on. In previous years, we had
thrown a big, catered fireworks display with all the elements of your
best commercial-grade show. This year, however, with us having been
out of town and the actual 4th happening mid-week, we had decided to
forego the show (much to our neighbor's dismay) and opt for a smaller
family celebration.

It felt weird to not be prepping for the big bash, but truth be
told, with the turn of events we had had with some of our friendships,
the season just didn't feel the same as it had in the past anyway. We
would still have a large group of people we loved show up for the party,
but some of our core friendships had fallen apart, and that made it seem
a little less celebratory. It had been a hard couple of years for us with
business, friendships, and all sorts of other messes. We've been people

who count our core friends as family, and when that trust is broken, it hurts! I realize that sometimes God has to close the door to some relationships in order to give us space to grow in others. But, I'm also human. It doesn't make it hurt any less.

While nearing home and scrolling through other's vacation pictures, summertime workout routines, pictures of their kids, snapshots of their dogs, and favorite 4th of July BBQ recipes, I stumbled across an absolute gem of an article that a friend shared by Rachel Macy Stafford discussing the "Invisible Mom" feeling. I read the article and related so much to the author's words that by the time I had finished, tears were streaming down my face. This was me. I was that invisible mom. Or at least how I felt at that moment.

The sense to be accepted is one of the most infuriating feelings I struggle with. I would love to shake it off, square my shoulders, and not give a damn whether the people like me, accept me, or even know I exist. But truth be told, I do, a lot. I like to be liked. I've never been a person who had a true group. I was raised Pentecostal but didn't fit in there because I didn't fully observe the dress code. In Elementary, I never fit in because I had come from a private school and only wore skirts. In Junior High, I transferred schools to a small country school where everyone had known each other their entire lives.

I married a man from a different small town where he and the entire community had grown up together, as had their parents, grandparents, and great grandparents. In small towns, everyone is "from somewhere" and has roots that trace back to this or that. My dad was from out of town. My mom had moved every six months of her life. I didn't graduate from my hometown school, and I didn't know the people of my husband's hometown. I had no true destination or origin, and as such, no pride or loyalty to an alma mater. The question of "Where I was of" became a bit of a sore subject. Each time I was asked, it became more clear I did not belong. And small towns, or at least the ones that I had had experience with, are not extremely open to outsiders. The fact I was the young girl who had married an older "successful" man did not necessarily make me easily welcomed. I remember hearing from a relative who worked in our bank about rumors I had married for money.

I just held my head high, squared my shoulders, and let the haters keep on hating. I didn't feel like an outsider due to the fact that I didn't look for acceptance from any of these people. I didn't need to fit in or belong amongst any group or clique. I had my truest sense of belonging with my family and those super tight core friends I loved like family. I had my people, and while I welcomed acquaintances, I wasn't looking to expand my inner circle. I knew people could only feel like outsiders if they were insecure enough to let it bother them, and I was content with the people I surrounded myself with. My family and friends were my happy place.

And, then, I stumbled upon this article. As I read it, the words resonated in so many ways. I started seeing class parties where the moms were all huddled up together while I was talking to the teachers. I started seeing mom lunches and girls' night outs I was not invited to. Loneliness crept in. With the loss of recent friendships, and two of my very best friends having moved out of town and out of state, I was just so lonely! My home that had always been my oasis where friends and loved ones had come to gather had started to feel lonely. We had gone through a difficult season with friendships, but we found there comes a time where you have to draw a line and move on. However, what's on the other side of that line may not be warm and welcoming. It might be downright lonely.

I couldn't decide why the article had struck me so deeply. I had just come from an incredible 10 day trip filled with all the warmth, love, family, and friendship I could ask for! How on earth could I feel so completely fulfilled and loved by my family and those around me while at the same time feeling so alone? Why had the need to fit in been such a struggle in my life? And, then, I realized, maybe I didn't feel like I fit in because I was never meant to fit in. Maybe I was meant to be different and make a difference. Maybe I was meant to stretch myself and reach others. Maybe fitting in felt comfortable. And if I was comfortable, I might not be fulfilling my purpose. I would love to tell you that it ended there. I'd love to tell you God told me it was okay, that I wasn't alone, and from that day forward I never once felt like I was in the weird space. But, I can't, because I'm human, flawed, and have an uncanny desire to be liked.

Several months later, I once again encountered that familiar feeling. I walked through the door and into the reception party filled with trepidation. My husband had a strong grip on my hand and gave me a smile as he opened the door. I knew there were a couple of people who wouldn't be thrilled to see me. People I had once loved and considered family. People I had done life with. People I missed dearly but had grown apart from. We were greeted by friends, gave them hugs, and quickly scanned the crowd. As we made our way through the people, I spotted my very best friend. We've literally been best friends for 33 years since the day she knocked on my door and asked if I wanted to come out to play. She's like a sister to me, and despite the fact we live approximately ten miles from each other, we very rarely have the opportunity to see each other. However, when we do see each other, watch out! We pick up exactly where we left off, and no one can get a word in edgewise. She had her back to me chatting with a group of girls I knew. One a friend from elementary, another an acquaintance I've spent time with, and the third, a friend of a friend's. All three girls I wouldn't necessarily consider friends, but also have no bad blood with. I came up behind her, grabbed her shoulders and leaned my face down in front of hers. She jumped up excitedly and greeted me with that big grin of hers, shouting it was the best night ever. She hugged me tight, and I soaked up all the love. And then, simultaneously as I stood there embraced by my lifelong friend in a bubble of love, I saw the temperature of the rest of the table over her shoulder. I saw the deep breath one of the girls took as she cut her eyes to the other and took a drink. I saw the second roll her eyes as she turned her head to the third, and then I watched the third as she breathed out heavily and turned her gaze away from us to stare in the opposite direction across the crowd. My friend was oblivious.

I made small talk with her as another girl walked up and joined our conversation, but I couldn't stay focused. What had just happened? What had I done to these people? What was the problem that I was completely unaware of? I spent the next hour and a half feeling uncomfortable and obsessing over the awkward encounter rather than being fully present and enjoying this rare occasion where I was able to spend time with my longtime friend. What a disservice I had done myself. I am constantly telling people around me to not care what others think of them. My kids know this to their very core. I teach people that the only opinion that matters is God's. However, at the end of the day, we're human, and the truth of the matter is it hurts. And sometimes people just suck for no apparent reason.

The crazy thing about a small town is it can feel like a fishbowl. I've watched it break other people. I've watched it send others into a lifetime of introverted hibernation because they would just rather not deal with life. It can make a difference of opinion with a tiny number of people feel like being shunned by an entire community. I'm a tough chick with a strong backbone (titanium actually) but, even I can only keep the face for so long. There are days it creeps in and tries to break me. On those days, I have to put myself in front of those who love me. I have to pour into my family and soul sisters. I have to pour into His Word and remind myself of whose child I am. I have to remind myself there is a great big world out there outside of the daily terrain I see, and it is filled with wonderful people.

That night, standing in the midst of that crowd, I was in the weird space. I'm a person you either love or hate. There just really isn't much of a take it or leave it with me. It truly comes down to the laws of attraction. A successful brand will be so well defined that it attracts the people who align with its values and repels those who don't. When a brand tries to be everything to everyone, that is when the lines get blurred, and the clear message isn't conveyed. I am the clearest representation of a brand that either attracts or repels you. I'm outspoken, brutally honest, and lack the ability to deal with BS or injustice. That doesn't always lend itself to being everyone's cup of tea. I am, in fact, a well-defined brand. I was standing there, in the presence of mutual love and adoration while also witnessing people's disdain for me. It sums up the current weird space I find myself in. With the podcast, I have found an incredible community of women from all over the world. They are mountain movers, servants, game-changers! They love big and love hard! They want to be a part of a bigger purpose and serve His people well! I have the distinct pleasure each week to interview these women. I hear their stories, get to know them, collect them, and keep them in my circle of mentors. They are people that influence me and encourage me. On the flip side, as I share the stories with the world, I have conversations with other women I know in person or only know via social media. They send me messages thanking me for what I'm doing. They share with me how an episode has impacted them. They tell me how my show has encouraged them to pursue their dreams. I run into these people in public and they share their excitement with me. I know in the grand scheme of things, my message is received in a positive manner. Sure, there are a few mean girls out there, but they're not the majority. I wish I didn't care. I really do. I've tried to convince myself over the years that I don't, but I do. Intellectually, I am completely aware of how ridiculous this is. But my heart. It's a different story.

I had one particular day that I was feeling down. I was lonely. I needed some time spent with girlfriends who could breathe new life into me. There was a Ladies Night in town that night, and I thought what the heck, I would call a couple of girlfriends and go shopping. I started the night off with the same prayer I find myself often uttering: "Dear Lord, please don't let me run into any mean girls tonight." We made our first stop at a vendor market and perused the different displays chatting with different ladies. The majority of the crowd knew each other, but one woman who I didn't know very well came up to me. I knew that I had worked with her older sister, but as she made her way over, I could not recall her name. I sat there, racking my brain as she eagerly exclaimed, "I just have to tell you; I love everything that you're doing on social media. I love The Power Project. I love your live videos. I love your business. Everything. I just love it all." And that's the point. The point has always been to reach *one* person sitting at home. The point is to inspire them, to empower them, and share with them what God wants me to share. That's what it's all about, not the haters! It's about that *one* person!

Why was I back in the stupid weird space? I had spent the morning scheduling podcast interviews and combing through Instagram to find women with inspiring stories. I examined their feeds, listened to their stories, and read their content. I considered if they aligned with my brand and if my listeners would enjoy their story. I quickly realized that I needed to reach out to my assistant because I needed to delegate that morning. She told me she would try to book some new guests for me but also told me she really thought my solo episodes were good, and I should start doing them every other episode. I could feel my anxiety creep in. The few solo episodes I had done, I procrastinated publishing each time until the very last minute. Then, once I did publish, I didn't promote them or share them with my network. I told her I hated my individual episodes and didn't feel like I brought enough to the table. She informed me she disagreed and thought it would give people a chance to get to know me more.

"You give talks all the time. You bring a lot to the table. You're knowledgeable in many fields of business, and I would personally love to hear more from you!" This kid… She's a dang genius. Have I mentioned she was 17 at the time? Man! I love her! I told her that would be fine and had her send me some topics to work on. And after we finished talking, I started thinking. Why was I so dang scared of solo episodes? When I first had the idea for a podcast, my goal was not actually to have guests each week. Originally, I wanted to launch the podcast because I wanted to speak into women. I was encountering so many women with limiting beliefs that didn't believe in themselves; I needed a way to show them anything was possible. I wanted to help them see themselves through God's eyes. I wanted to help women feel inspired to pursue their dreams. I wanted to equip them with the tools necessary to run businesses. I wanted to coach them through the ups and downs of life. I wanted to empower them and let them know that I believe in them. I wanted to have open, honest conversations where I pushed them to be the best versions of themselves. I wanted to have tough talks where we tackled topics of navigating parenting, marriage, business, volunteering, and following God's will. I have all of these conversations in my head daily. So, why had I given my platform away?

Don't get me wrong, I love spotlighting other women! I love teaching women that there's room for all of us at the table. I love lifting other women up and showing the world that we as women don't have to compete with each other. I love sharing other women's stories. But this platform began because God Gave ME a Voice. Uniquely mine for me to share with the world. And, instead, I had been hiding behind other women's stories. Was it because I felt less than? Was it because I didn't feel like I added value or didn't feel like I had accomplished enough?

Nope. Plain and simple. It was because I could hear the mean girls in my head and didn't want to be judged. I was literally letting a handful of people dictate the value that I brought to the world. How dare I make their opinions greater than God's call on my life?

I found myself once again walking into yet another room full of people celebrating. This time, I said hello to everyone, grabbed a mimosa, and made small talk. I looked around at the pretty decorations, perfectly styled outfits, and smiling faces. I couldn't believe how long it had been since I had seen several of the faces. I caught up with friends, played with babies, and listened to conversations. I chatted with one friend and mentioned the book to her, which she was so eager to hear more about. We talked about the upcoming hat company and all the things going on. It felt great to put all the words out into the world. I wasn't thinking about these things. I was actually doing them. I smiled to myself and took a sip of my drink as I gazed around the room. It was so pretty, everyone was so happy, and my book was about to become a reality...

How to Pursue Your Purpose in Spite of the Haters:

1. Know your worth. Place a legitimate value on what you bring to the table.

2. Recognize that it is about them (mindset, insecurities, self-belief, etc.) and not you.

3. Appreciate the people who support you and let them know how grateful you are for them.

4. Eliminate people from your life (and on social media) who make you feel bad.

5. Nurture the relationships that make you feel like a better person, and spend intentional time with those people.

CHAPTER 15

Growing Pains

Here's the one thing about a purpose journey no one really tells you. Not everyone in your life is going to jump on that bandwagon with you as eagerly or quickly as you did. Just like your parenting journey or your success in business, personal development doesn't happen at the same time for everyone in your circle. And, more importantly, the timeline of your husband's spiritual growth journey isn't going to look the same as yours. When my husband and I met, I was not following God's call for my life. I won't say I was far from God, because I've never felt that in my life. Even in the midst of rebellion and running from God, I have always talked to Him and always felt His presence in my life.

However, I wasn't doing anything to bring glory to Him. Our relationship was based on fun, fun and a mutual respect for one another. We understood each other's brains. We had spent a great deal of time together before we ever dated and knew how similar our outlooks on life were. We were two different people but were incredibly compatible in life and had a great friendship. My husband had a nickname, and I didn't actually know his real name for two years. Once we began dating, I asked what he preferred me to call him. He informed me the nickname was not his name, and he had never actually appreciated it. This man was 37 years old, and people had been calling him this nickname since he was 14. Twenty-three years and he had never stood up and said, "Hey man, don't call me that!" Even his own brother and nieces and nephews called him by his nickname. I was blown away he wouldn't have voiced his opinion before, and immediately started calling him by his actual name. I, being the incredibly outspoken one in the relationship, couldn't imagine letting anyone call me anything I didn't wish them to. This should have been my first clue into his difficulty with communicating his feelings.

As much as we enjoyed each other's company, we also had some obvious differences. I'll never forget having a conversation one day where I summed something up so directly he exclaimed, "Man! Where were you ten years ago? You could have saved me a lot of trouble in life!" I thought for a moment, and then laughingly replied, "Um, junior high!" There is a large age difference between my husband and me, but I've never been concerned with age. I didn't go looking for someone older; it just happened. I had spent my entire life hanging out with people older than me. All throughout school, kids my age annoyed me. I was an old soul and had been a deep thinker from a very young age. In Kindergarten, I attended the private church school my aunt and mom volunteered at. My babysitter was in high school, and I would hang out with her any chance I got. I remember sitting with her and her friends at lunch one day when my aunt came up and told me I needed to sit with kids my own age because these girls were too mature for me. What? Didn't she know these were my friends? I was so annoyed. At most family functions or social gatherings, you could find me at a table with the ladies. I wasn't concerned with the play of children. I would much rather listen to the womenfolk. Plus, if I was lucky, I might gather a little church gossip. So, it really just made sense that I ended up with someone older.

Although we were so compatible in so many ways, we were also two very different people with very different upbringings. Age was not our biggest difference by far. It's crazy when your heart falls in love. You don't think, how will we raise our children? What church will we attend? How was this man raised? Was he taught to be a spiritual leader? Was he taught how to openly express his feelings? Was he raised with confidence in Christ? Will he be able to raise confident, Christian children? What are his insecurities? How will this play out in our marriage?

I can tell you the exact moment I fell deeply and madly in love with my husband. We were out with friends celebrating a birthday party at a very large, very loud, very crowded club. This was one of those places with four separate rooms, separate DJ's, separate dance floors, restaurants... We had a table with all of our friends, and everyone kept coming and going from the dance floor, yelling over each other and having a great time. The two of us sat, staring at each other, and whispering in each other's ears for the entire night. We might as well have been the last two people on the earth. It was just him and me. I knew it. Right there. He leaned over and whispered in my ear, "You know if it weren't for my previous history, I'd marry you tomorrow." I whispered back, "And if it weren't for mine, I'd say yes." There we were, two broken individuals with enough baggage for a couple of checked bags and carry-ons, falling in love, in the midst of a loud, crowded nightclub. I can hear the music and almost feel sparkles from the disco ball falling down around us. I think back to that moment often. Was there free will? Absolutely. Do I believe this was God's divine plan to save each of us from our own stubborn selves? One hundred percent. This man was meant for me, and I was created for him.

So why does it sometimes seem so hard? Why are there so many differences between the two of us we struggle with? Why does it so often feel like work? It's really quite simple. We are two messed up individuals in need of a savior. We cannot solely put faith in each other and depend only on one another. We have to depend on Jesus to sustain our marriage. Also, we're the absolute most hard-headed individuals you will ever meet. Proverbs 27:17-- "as iron sharpens iron, so does one man to another..."-- is the mantra of our marriage. I tell him constantly I'm sharp enough, mind because they can quit already. It didn't take long for me to realize the fun of our relationship and our shared common interests did not mean we were always on the same page. We were far from being on the same page with some of the really big topics.

When I was expecting our first child, we had to have a conversation. My husband was raised Catholic, attended a Catholic school, and thus went to mass every single day. I knew he was non-practicing and hadn't attended church since I had known him. I didn't have a church at the time and was pretty burned-out on religion as well. However, I knew I wanted my baby to be brought up in a home where his parents knew God, and he was taught about Jesus. "I don't believe in all that religion crap. I don't think prayer works, and I'm never going to go to church with you, so don't ask," he told me. It probably should have been a conversation before we started a family together. At the time, I was not walking in God's will and was far from obedient, but I knew I wanted to eventually get back to it, just not in the way I had previously known church. It was too flawed by man. I wanted something pure. Like I said, I was never without God. I knew God and talked to him regularly. But I didn't know how to serve him on Earth without it being convoluted with organized religion and man's law. And now, here I was with a man who had zero intentions of being the spiritual leader in our house.

I floated through a few years of attending church on the major holidays: Christmas, Easter, and the occasional Mother's Day. My husband, much to my surprise, came with me, but this was merely a traditional appearance. Shortly after the birth of our second child, I knew I wanted to start attending church regularly with my babies. Around this same time, one of our wildest and craziest party animal friends had gone through a divorce. He had been blind-sided by it and was incredibly depressed. In his search for healing, he found Jesus. He found peace and healing at a non-denominational church and was even baptized. I decided that if this church could lead this wild child to salvation, it had to be the right church for me. I started going with the kids and never asked my husband to join. My stepson was 15 at the time, and on the weekends we had him, he went with the little boys and me..

This church was unlike any I had ever attended. It felt like home when I walked through the doors. While the pastor spoke about sin, it wasn't hellfire and brimstone. Grace was taught. Mercy. Love. Servanthood. It felt so right and so refreshing to hear God's word taught at such a simple level. While we weren't involved with serving the church or even in the community, it was what I needed at the time. The church was about 45 minutes from my house, so I didn't have friends or community members I attended with. In all honesty, I liked the anonymity of it. Having grown up in a church where everybody knew everybody else's business, it was refreshing to walk in, check the kids into Sunday school, grab a seat, and just listen to God's word. One morning, while getting ready for church, my husband began getting dressed as well. I walked into the room and with a confused face, looked at him and asked what he was doing. He shrugged his shoulders, "I thought I would go to church with you and the kids today." I had been attending for close to two years at that point and had never expected him to join me. I nonchalantly nodded my head, told him okay, and walked out of the room. Looking back, I don't know I even realized God's hand in my life here. I knew it was huge and thanked God, but I can now see the plan so much more clearly. After church that day, he told me "he could "do that church." He liked the laid-back manner and the simple depiction of truth. We attended for a few years off and on but were never fully engaged in the church.

As life got busy and kids got older, church on Sunday became less of a necessity. We still hit it up on the important days and the occasional "nothing else is going on Sunday." We continued that pattern for a few years until we found ourselves in our current church I mentioned earlier in this book which literally helped to save our marriage. I would love to tell you that after four years, he is obediently serving and is the spiritual leader of our household. However, that is not the case. I am an achiever and activator. I thrive on seeing goals and dreams come to fruition. I have this beautiful vision of my husband standing next to me on a stage, sharing his testimony after submitting his life to God whole-heartedly. But the truth is, that will most likely never happen. Not that I don't believe he will have a beautiful testimony to share, but he doesn't want any part of a platform of any type. And, he's terrified of public speaking, so the chance of me having our dream fulfilled of us being a power couple is slim to none. The truth is my dreams for him are not what matter. All that matters is his relationship with Christ and what he is called to do. That is the thing about salvation and calling. No one else's journey is in anyone else's control. It is all in God's hands. He offers salvation and issues the call, but whether each person chooses to accept it is up to that individual person.

Our purpose is the gift God gives to each of us. Whether or not we choose to lean in and unwrap it fully is of our own free will. We can't control what other people do with their calling in life, even if we are so intimately entwined. What we can only control is our own devotion, time spent in prayer, and personal actions. Also, we have to remember to give praise and worship for the steps of faith we see those around us take in life. I can't control how quickly my husband steps into his purpose in life, but I am grateful for where he is today. That same man who told me he would never attend church with me, sits each Sunday listening to our pastor with his arm draped around my shoulders. He gives an offering monthly, which is huge for him, considering it took him a while to get over the "all churches are greedy and just want your money" mindset. When I suggest serving the survivors I mentor with a day visit, he gladly prepares all the food and cheerfully hosts alongside me. He fervently prepares his prize-winning pot of chili for the chili cookout each year, and eagerly awaits the Father's Day Car Show. I never take for granted the ways I see God working in his life. I use him as an example, but this applies to anyone in your life you are wishing to be further along the path. Make sure you are grateful for how far God has brought them today.

None of this means I stop hoping, praying, and speaking into him. It doesn't mean I quit urging him to step into God's calling and see himself through the eyes of his Creator. In the same manner he has pushed me to step outside of my comfort zone in business or take risks in life, I will keep urging him to let go of the safety of shore and step out into the water with me. And, I will always and forever hold him to a higher standard because we were not meant to stay stagnant in life. We are meant to grow, to flourish, to lean deeper into God's understanding. This is the sign of a healthy relationship. Do you push each other to be the best version of yourselves? This can apply to marriages or friendships. And, it's important to remember, while we are urging others around us to be more, we must be leaning into the areas we need to improve as well. I battle my own internal struggle daily where I yearn for my husband to be the spiritual leader of our household, while I find myself simultaneously not wanting to submit. Submission just does not come naturally to me, in the same manner, leading does not come naturally for him. I have to remind myself often he is a baby Christian, unlike myself, who was born and raised on a church pew, and have known Jesus since I was five-years-old. I gave my life to Christ at age nine and have had a deep relationship with him ever since. Then God reminds me he has been pursuing me for my entire life, and I have just recently begun to submit. It literally took me 34 years before I finally asked God what He wanted me to do. And so, I must remember to be patient and trust his ways are greater than mine even when the control freak in me wants everything done on my schedule and according to my terms.

I began digging deep into encouraging my husband to lead without nagging him. Not just spiritual leadership, but our tendency to have reversed leadership roles. It's my innate ability to lead, and his willingness to let me. I'm sure I set the precedent years ago. If a date night was going to happen, I would arrange the sitter, make the reservations, look up directions, lay out his clothes, and fix his hair. Vacation? I had every single detail lined out to the point, mind because they would not only not know the itinerary, but the actual destination as well. Family schedule? I have always organized it, put it in the calendar and synced it to his phone. Doctor's visits, family holidays, social gatherings, all scheduled by me. And so, for the longest time, I just thought this was how it was meant to be in our relationship. I knew how to lead. I'm good at it. I've done it all my life. I'll keep doing it. But it started to create friction when my husband tried to lead, but I didn't allow him. The kids are the most common place where this happens. At this point in my boys' lives, it's time for them to see their dad as the leader. They are no longer my babies. They are becoming men and need to be taught how to lead as men. But each time my husband tries to lead, I inevitably intervene. He steps into the role of authoritarian, and because I feel he is not leading spiritually, I don't allow him to lead in the parental role either. "I know better. I'm wiser. I have more grace. I'll take care of my kids." These are the thoughts that keep me from letting him take the lead. It's a constant struggle I see play out in not just our lives but others' as well.

I have had this conversation with both Christian women and non-believers. We wives yearn for our husbands to exemplify leadership but don't allow it. Often times, when we are so focused on how our husband is not leading, we overlook the fact we are not submitting either. Girls, I get it! We don't want to submit. We are empowered women. We want to quote all the other parts of the bible, "So ought men to love their wives as their own bodies… He that loveth his wife loveth himself…." We could endlessly wax on poetically about all the ways that God called men to lead their wives. But, listen up. We have a spiritual obligation to submit. "Now as the church submits to Christ, so also wives should submit in everything to their husbands" (Ephesians 5:24). The bible does not say "If your husband is doing everything right and walking in God's call, submit to him." It simply says to submit. I just lost 80% of my readers right now. Do not close this book yet. Keep reading, I promise, there is a silver lining.

Most of the time, when we women find ourselves leading a marriage, it is by default because he hasn't stepped into the leadership role. Not always, but often this is the case. There are many other underlying issues, but I personally believe this is the most common. There are ways we can personally change that trajectory. It comes down to the power of submission. I hate that word. My teeth are clenched right now. But power lies in submission. Have you ever watched a puppy bound up to a larger older dog excitedly wanting to play, only to be greeted by bared teeth and a growl? The puppy instantly rolls over on its back, paws in the air, while looking super cute and lovable, and then before you know it, the two are frolicking around the yard as if they are best friends. The puppy rolled over as a signal to say, "I get it big guy, you are the top-dog around here." However, you also saw the puppy take control of the situation. The puppy won the old dog over and got him to play with him, which was what he ultimately wanted in the first place. What if through submission, prayer, praise, and partnership you could help your husband accept his role as leader?

Something else I have witnessed along this purpose journey is the enemy will try to tell you any lie in order to have you believe your growth is not a good thing. He'll try to convince you your marriage is dying because of your growth. You'll start to believe you're growing apart, and you're not sure how you can both be on the same page. That voice in your head will start telling you don't have anything in common anymore. One partner is digging deep to show up as the best version of themselves, and the other may appear to be stagnant. You'll see all the work you're putting in and feel somewhat resentful you're not both on the same page. I've seen this both in my own marriage and in the lives of many other women around me. I've seen women listen to that voice and throw their marriages away in the name of becoming the best version of themselves. You have to shut that down. You have to become so focused on you and your walk you're not concerned with anyone else's. You have to love your spouse for who they are but focus on your own walk.

I know the pain of the enemy attacking your most intimate relationships. I know the strife, the struggle, and the desire for the one you love most intimately on this planet to truly understand what it feels like to walk in the purpose they were created for. I know the overwhelming joy of stepping into your calling while simultaneously experiencing the isolation of others not understanding. I don't believe God has us walk through these times for us to endure undue pain. I believe He has us walk through these times to become more dependent upon Him. The stronger our relationship with Him becomes, the more strength we can bring to the relationships around us. We learn to love with grace and mercy so those around us can witness the earthly demonstration of Jesus's love for us. We learn to let those closest to us walk their own purpose journey while we focus on our own. And, for those we are hoping will join us on this journey, we can learn to never give up because Jesus didn't give up on us. It's hard. It's work. No one said following God would make everything in your life easy. From experience, I can tell you, the more intentional you become about being obedient and following God's will to fulfill your purpose, the more the enemy chases you. The more he takes the most intimate relationships in your life and tries to tear them to shambles. The more he makes you doubt yourself and your capabilities. The more isolated you feel from those around you. I have found myself in the midst of a storm telling God I am tired. I've told Him, "I'm tired of being strong. I'm tired of leading. I'm tired. I need to be carried. I need to be nurtured. I need someone to be strong for me." And then, God reminds me, He is that. He is my strength. He is my fortress. He is my calm in the midst of the storm. Everything around me may feel like a battle, but He sent His Son to wage war for my soul. He wants me to surrender and lean on Him, mind because they can help me fight my battles, and in doing so, I'm allowed to love my husband where he is at. I am allowed to grow into the person God is calling me to be and lead by example. And, in doing so, I have been able to see God at work in my marriage and my husband's life. I have been able to see my husband lean into God's call for his life and begin to seek out his own purpose journey. And, I've witnessed my husband taking steps to become the leader God has created him to be.

Does surrendering to God make everything else easy? No. Do I still have days where I feel like I am on island in the midst of a hurricane? Absolutely. When I find myself on that island, unable to see through the waves whatever lesson may lie on the other side of the storm, He is still there. In the midst of the storm, all I know is that I do not want this to be part of my journey. But when the waves die down and the skies clear I can typically look back and see why the storm was necessary. The Big Island of Hawaii is the youngest island in the chain, and as a result, has the smallest beaches with coarse sand and the most dramatic drop-offs into the Pacific Ocean. Other islands in the chain such as Maui, have long gradual sloping beaches with finer granules of sand. This is because over time the waves crashing along the islands erode the volcanic rock and carry the sediment out to sea. As years pass and the waves crash back and forth, the edges of the sediment become less sharp, and the drop-offs become more of a gradual slope. There are times I needed to be standing on that island in the midst of the storm for parts of my life to be eroded by the crashing waves. I can stand today, feet planted in the serenity of the beach knowing I, too, have been forged by the storm.

Despite the obstacles and storms along your path, it is all part of his greater purpose for your life. Does it come with infinitesimal challenges along the way? Absolutely. Friends, family, relationships, illness, finances... these are all challenges that will inevitably arise and derail each of us at times. But we can't be so focused on the daily struggle that we forget how far God has brought us. Even I, standing on the sandy beach looking out into the sea, have to remember to take my sunglasses off and look back. Look back and see how the storms have shaped you for this journey.

How to Let Your Husband Lead:

1. Encourage (don't nag) your husband to take the lead.

2. Cover him with words of life, strength, and affirmation about his leadership skills.

3. Submit to him. Allow him to make decisions you would typically make.

4. Thank him when he does lead (and don't critique the way that he led).

5. Share with him how it makes you feel when he leads.

Those Who Wait Upon the Lord

I've spent my entire life waiting impatiently. When I was little, I had this overwhelming sense of urgency in my soul. I literally thought Jesus was going to come back before I could fulfill my purpose. I just wanted to grow up and accomplish things! I couldn't wait to grow up. I couldn't wait to start my period and wear a bra. I couldn't wait to get a driver's license, so I was never at the mercy of anyone else when I wanted to go places. I couldn't wait to get a job to have my own money. I couldn't wait to graduate high school and college, so I could fulfill my purpose. And, I couldn't wait to turn 30. I had looked forward to it my entire life. I had been told I was too young for so many years I couldn't wait to be older and wiser, so people would take me seriously. But then a crazy thing happened. I turned 30 and suddenly felt like I had missed out. I had spent the last seven years as a housewife raising babies. I had loved every minute of it, but I had a purpose to fulfill. I started brainstorming things I could do. I did the three-day, 60-mile walk. Not because I was personally attached to the cause but simply because it was something bigger than me I could be attached to. And, I waited a few more years on the purpose thing.

Several more years later, and I am still struggling with waiting upon the Lord. I'm a purpose-driven achiever. I like an action plan. I know my calling in life. I know my purpose. I know my end goal is to be an international speaker who inspires people to lead purpose-filled lives and own their God-given power. However, I struggle with patiently waiting upon the Lord. I know it is all in His timing. I have the innate ability to become so focused on the destination I forget I am not in control of the journey.

I've consciously been waiting upon the Lord and listening for his next direction for my life for the past two and a half years. This past summer, my family took a far from pleasant vacation. However, while we were traveling back, God gave me the advice I needed.

I was reading in my Bible, studying my devotional, and journaling when I read Isaiah 40:31— "Those who wait upon the Lord shall renew their strength and mount up with wings like eagles." If you are willing to be utterly dependent, He will enable you to do all He has called you to do. I took my pen out and drew Eagle's wings on each side of the word 'ambassador' on my wrist. I feel I am called to be an ambassador of truth, an ambassador of inspiration, an ambassador of motivation, an ambassador for Christ. In retrospect, this word has been spoken over me for years. In college, I had had dreams of being a United Nations ambassador. At A21's 10-year celebration, while discussing my role in the organization with a staff member, he suggested I be an ambassador. I googled, "What does the Bible say about public speaking?" Ephesians 6:19-20 states, "That words may be given to me in opening of my mouth boldly to proclaim the mystery of the gospel for which I am an Ambassador...that I may declare it boldly as I ought to speak." Ambassador is my word. I added the wings to remind myself to wait on Him to fulfill my calling.

I then went back to my journal to write the scripture down. We were traveling back from what would go down in our family history book as quite possibly the most awful vacation we had ever taken. The unfortunate series of events that had transpired over the course of the eight days could only be rivaled by that of a Chevy Chase family vacation. Each time something went wrong, I just kept reminding myself there would be some sort of meaning or purpose or something that would make this hellacious nightmare make sense one day. Oh, $3,000 of repair costs for our new motorhome paid to the local shady mechanic without the unit being repaired? Well, maybe Phil's family was struggling, and God used us to bless him. Twenty-five hours of sitting in a truck stop parking lot with a broken-down motorhome while the rest of our family was on a beach? Maybe we were placed there to speak into Billy, the truck driver, and remind him to chase his dreams. Our motorhome being stuck at the repair center for two days? Maybe that service writer that wanted to know all about my work in the fight against human trafficking needed the name of an organization that could help her or a loved one. My oldest cut his knee wide open, but of course, the country pharmacy did not have butterfly bandages. So, my emotionally and physically exhausted body walked up to the counter to ask the pharmacist if they were hidden there. As she began helping me, with a furrowed brow, and discerning face, she looked up and asked, "You're Brandi, right?" Right there in the middle of Nowhere, Tennessee. I stared at her for a solid five seconds trying to decide what Twilight Zone hole I had slipped into that someone 842 miles from my home would know me. The podcast? Instagram? Facebook? As I drove back to camp, I thought to myself how, for some reason, I was meant to be at that pharmacy counter at that very moment. I was meant to run into that girl; I just couldn't dream up the answer yet. Maybe she was a reminder that people are watching the way we react to life. At my wits' end with this vacation, I could have been irate and lost my mind because they didn't have butterfly bandages, but instead, I was gracious and took the recommendations she made. Maybe this was God telling me people are paying attention to my behavior, so I should make sure that I'm not only talking the talk but walking the walk.

So, there we were with a motorhome that was on again off again with a working engine, and we desperately needed to just get back to Texas and close this chapter. And here we sat for two straight hours in *stopped* traffic on a closed mountain highway, a full-on road rage scenario happening in front of us that came incredibly close to someone being shot by a truck-driver, and my anxiety at the absolute highest point one can get to before it turns into an actual pulmonary embolism. I had tried so hard to keep everything together for everyone else on this trip and not lose my cool that I hadn't even thought to take a moment to check in with myself and breathe. I had been preoccupied with making sure the kids had fun, and the trip wasn't miserable for them. I had taken a great deal of care trying to keep my husband calm so that he didn't ruin the rest of the trip for everyone else. And, in full disclosure, I thought he might possibly have a heart attack before it was all over. I had spent countless hours on the phone with manufacturers, warranty repair, and service technicians trying to remedy the situation. And, I had continued to make lodging, dinner, and sightseeing arrangements all the while. It's no wonder I had the ever so familiar feeling of an anxiety attack. My chest was tight, my breathing was rapid, and my nerves were wound tighter than a long-tailed cat in a room full of rocking chairs. Any acceleration or stop my husband made sent me into a sudden fit of panic. I had reverted to what I know best when nervous or anxious, control. I was nagging every single mile along this painstakingly long journey home. At this rate, we were going to either kill each other or end up divorced before we got home. So rather than risk either of those two happening, I decided it would be best to read the Bible, journal a bit, study my devotional, and try with all my might to accept the things I could not change and relinquish full control into the hands of God.

In the midst of reading about God's strength renewing us, being called to be an ambassador, and relinquishing control, I was still finding time to yell at my husband for following the other vehicles too closely. As I neared the point of no return, I read Isaiah 40:31. I wrote it down. Then, I read some more and thought, "I know my calling, I just have to wait. He will enable those who wait upon him. I will be renewed. I will mount up with wings as eagles." I wrote, "Those that wait upon the Lord--" But suddenly the breaks were slammed on, and I look up to see us coming dangerously close to kissing the truck's bumper ahead of us. As I opened my mouth to yell at my husband, I was stopped by a large blue square reading 'Isaiah 40:31 TRUST' on the back of that truck's bumper. "*That's my scripture!*" I proclaimed.

Being incredibly confused with why I wasn't yelling at him and what scripture exactly I was talking about, my husband questioned me, "What? What scripture!"

"My scripture! The one I am writing down right now at this very minute!" I looked back at my wrist. I had never in my life had the most clearly stated affirmation of what God wanted me to do as in that very moment of my life. I decided then I would no longer question his plans. I would wait upon the Lord, and I would be an ambassador for Him.

But, how do you wait upon the Lord? I had been waiting. I had said yes over two years early. Life is short. I needed to get the show on the road! But how? How does one even go about such a thing? I heard this all my life but couldn't think of a time that anyone had truly explained how to actually wait upon the Lord. Patience is a virtue… I knew that. I also knew it was one I struggled dearly with. Nonetheless, I was committed to waiting. As we rolled down the road, the engine sensor lights flashed on once again. This was our signal to take a break in hopes that we could get the lights off and resume our trek home.

A song by the band Mumford & Sons popped into my head, and I googled it. As I read the words, I was shocked to learn that this was a song about waiting upon the Lord. As I read on about breaking my step and Him forgiving and me not forgetting, my mind landed on the last verse of the song, "Raise my hands, paint my spirit gold, and bow my head, keep my heart slow."

I wrote the four requests down. I immediately felt this was the actual instruction I had been looking for. These were the four prayers I could dig deeper into in order to take action in the waiting process. I would ask him to raise my hands, paint my spirit gold, bow my head, and keep my heart slow. But, what would that look like scripturally?

How I Wait Upon the Lord:

- RAISE MY HANDS

  Psalm 34:1— "I will bless the Lord at all times; his praise shall continuously be in my mouth." At all times. In the good and the bad. When we were stuck in a truck stop parking lot in the middle of nowhere with a brokedown motorhome. I will praise Him and thank Him. I will ask Him daily to raise my hands so that even when I don't feel like praising, He will call me to. And, when I have more pressing issues and actual real problems in life if I am unable to raise my hands, I ask that he will raise them for me.

- PAINT MY SPIRIT GOLD

  Matthew 5:16— "In the same way, let your light shine before others that they may see your good deeds and glorify your Father in Heaven." I would ask Him to daily paint my spirit gold so that His light would shine through me. In every situation. Through the trials and with those I come in contact with, my prayer would be that His light would radiate so brightly that they would be able to see Him in me even in the midst of my flawed human nature.

- BOW MY HEAD

  Matthew 9:18— "A ruler came in and knelt before him saying, "My daughter has just died, but come and lay your hand on her, and she will live."

  Mark 5:6-7— "He ran and fell down before him and crying out with a loud voice, he said, "What have you to do with me, Jesus, Son of the Most High God? I adjure you by God, do not torment me."

  Luke 5:12— "There came a man full of leprosy. And when he saw Jesus, he fell on his face and begged him, "Lord if you will, you can make me clean."

  All of these men bowed before Jesus in expectation. They boldly went before Him and made their request known. I would bow my head and clearly take my ask to Him.

- KEEP MY HEART SLOW

  Philippians 4:6-7— "Do not be anxious about anything, but in everything by prayer and supplication with thanksgiving let your requests be made known to God. And the peace of God, which surpasses all understanding, will guard your hearts and your minds in Jesus Christ." This was the big one for me. It is so simple to recite these words, but in a time where it is easy to be pulled in a million different directions, it is much more difficult to put this scripture into action. This would be a daily mantra of mine to help me keep my anxiety at bay and remember that His peace surpasses all understanding.

I've always considered the waiting upon the Lord as a passive process. As an achiever and activator, this is difficult. I have always felt the need for something to do while I waited. And so, I had this new process of actively waiting upon the Lord. I vowed to follow his call as He continued to fulfill His purpose for my life.

Birthing a Social Enterprise

O ct. 18, 2018:

My girlfriend, in a group text with another girlfriend: Good Morning! Okay, so before you think I'm crazy, let me explain... I'm listening to the audible of Imperfect Courage today, and in Ch. 9, she is talking about the success stories of artisans and the sisterhood effect. I had thought-what if we started something like this for traffic victims? To give them a fresh start. Teach them some type of craft and sell their products. Train them to sew, make jewelry, or bake? What do y'all think?

My message: Okay, I've been hammering out details this morning for The Power Hat Company: Hats that give back, made by survivors and company ran by survivors, because more than donations, or percentages of sales. I need job solutions for survivors that not only gives them a fulfilling career but also a sense of purpose. The girls are not going to stay focused when they're working at McDonald's for minimum wage but know how they can make a couple hundred in a night…. It would be a social enterprise. The girls would learn a skill, have a job, and give back. I would base it in Denton with the opportunity of expanding. No storefronts, just online sells because e-commerce is where it's at. I think I can get a partnership with A21 to help with grants or something. And, I know that I have boutiques that support the cause and will carry them.

C: Oh good! That's the exact thing I was thinking! WTG Brandi! Let me know if you ever need help with it. I will do whatever you need. Bookkeeping, etc…

Me: Shut up! You're going to be a founding member! Welcome to the mountain moving club! God's timing is impeccable! There are a lot of companies that support trafficking, but I haven't found a hat company. And, y'all know I LOVE hats! I had thought about a coffee shop, but there's a lot of coffee shops supporting the cause too!

C: I'm crying right now! That is so awesome! I should've known you were already on it! I'm in an online meeting not paying any attention, trying to brainstorm right now to think of some product that hasn't been done—then there you go! Awesome idea!

Me: Dude! I came up with the idea last night to start a hat line. Literally, this morning, while listening to my own podcast with Kyra Anachkova, that it should be a social enterprise for survivors in NTX… and, then you texted! You're in Sister! I always talk about how I wear a lot of hats (figuratively) but I also do literally. Remember, Tiff, me saying I wanted to do a shoot with all my different hats for a blog post? People always tell me they wish they could pull off hats like I do, and I always tell them they can, that they just have to have the confidence and own it. SO, people have started taking pics of themselves in new hats and tagging me in them, telling me I inspired them. I bought this funky olive green felt hat with a feather the day before yesterday. I've had probably six conversations about it since and how I can pull hats off. I started thinking about how I love hats of all kinds. My vision is to have all the types of hats: fedoras, ball caps, homburgs, panamas, etc… hats for anyone. So, I sat there trying to decide execution for the process and thinking that I need someone detail oriented to come alongside because I'm an achiever but have to have the detail person that can handle all the mundane crap that wears me out… and I have a lot of shit going on right now: The Power Hat Company: Hats with a Purpose Owned by Women Empowering and Restoring.

C: I agree! I absolutely love this! This will go so far! I agree with you, unless these women can make an actual living, they can't/won't ever get out. A friend of mine worked with Friends of The Family when we were in college. I learned so much! It's such a sad thing!

Oct. 19, 2018

Me: Okay, so I've been researching hat makers to find a company that would consider partnering with me. Possibly apprenticing the survivors in the actual making part of the process. Because, I really want their hands to be involved in the creation piece so that they can learn a skill. And, I found this company and was super stoked, especially since they're local. But, the town is actually a town in England!

C: Well, we could go to England! I was trying to think last night, there was an old hat maker around the area years ago. I'm going to ask around to see who it was.

T: What an awesome sign from God that you're going to flourish into the only American hat company keeping survivors employed!

Me: There's a lady in Dallas with a major international customer base… she might be interested in at least letting someone apprentice under her. I want the main focus to be fashion hats, because those are the ones that no one thinks they can pull off: floppy hats, fedoras, etc… And, as far as baseball caps, I want them all to be statement hats with a power word: FREE, POWERFUL, FORGIVEN, RESTORED, LOVED, EMPOWERED, CHOSEN, REDEEMED…

C: Y'all are so good with envisioning the whole picture! I love this! Those are great power words!

Me: So, here's the thing…. I HAVE to finish this book by 12/31…. so, I have to push this off until at least January. But, I have brought it up with my friends at A21 and the RFW director. But I have to table it for now.

T: Write sista, WRITE!!!

C: Yes! Focus on that!

And so, the topic was tabled. My book, obviously, was not finished by December 31st. I decided my word for 2019 was FOCUS. I pick a word each year. In 2017, it was Purpose. In 2018, it was Reach. 2019, focus. Why Focus? Because when you are a purpose-driven achiever as well as an activator, you can tend to sprint from one thing to the next and spread yourself incredibly thin. In 2018, I had all but abandoned my skincare business and team. I had decided that it was more important to focus on the non-profit work I was doing rather than continue building my business. However, what I seemed to forget was I had a team who still relied on me, and I had customers who had placed the fate of their skin in my hands. So, for 2019, I would recommit to my business and focus. I would also focus on growing my podcast. What had been launched very quickly and somewhat haphazardly needed more intentional focus placed on it. And, I needed to focus on finishing my book. Because, everyone kept asking me when I was going to write a book. So, I thought really hard about writing some more.

However, if I'm completely honest, up until August, I had written just 1,900 words. While strategizing with my assistant over social media growth and engagement, podcast downloads, organic reach, and speaking engagements, she offered some wise advice delivered via millennial style, "You just need to finish that book bro. I think the rest will work itself out after that." I attended a personal development conference a little over one month before, and while at the conference had the overwhelming urge to finish my book. We had written down the ten dreams, selected one dream as our number one goal, and mapped out action steps for achieving that dream. "My book is a NY Times #1 Best Seller". I circled it. Then I looked at the roadmap of achieving that dream. Well, here is where it started. Finishing the dang book. For too long, I had told people I'm working on a book. It was time to actually finish and publish a book. And so, I wrote.

Since I had committed to focusing on the book, each morning in my journal, under "The goal I'm going to achieve first" I had been writing, "finish my book, I am writing daily to finish my book, publish my book, finish my book." On August 13th, I wrote "finish my book, Oct. 18th deadline" next to it and highlighted the date. I charted the word count and did the math on roughly how many words per day I needed to write in order to have the book completed by the deadline. That seemed super feasible. I can whip out a few thousand words pretty quickly. I had renewed confidence that I might actually complete that goal.

August 14th, 2019: Met a friend of mine for dinner I had met at a speaking engagement earlier in the year:

She is a transformational life coach, and we both are super passionate about living purpose-filled lives. From the moment I saw her walk into the event last spring, wearing fabulous, blush-colored party pants, I knew that we were destined to work together again. After we chatted backstage and wrapped up the evening, we exchanged contact information with the intent of collaborating in the future. With the kids getting back in school, it was a great time to meet up and discuss vision casting for 2020. We discussed God's calling, our purpose in life, obstacles we've had to overcome, and eventually landed on her big picture vision of working with non-profits. I shared my vision to start The Power Hat Company. I'm not even sure why I shared it with her because I hadn't moved forward with the idea since the year before. Well, aside from purchasing way too many hats and noting the brands I most liked. She thought the idea was awesome, especially since she, too, is a big fan of hats!

The director of the aftercare home had asked me to teach a weekly business class. It was a class to help prepare the girls for gainful employment attached to purpose outside of the house. Since most of these girls have never had "legal" jobs, there is a lot of work to do within the class. When she first reached out, I was hesitant. I wasn't sure if I had the time to invest in teaching a class each week again. I had the deadline of the book looming and was working furiously to finish writing. I asked if I could have a couple of days to think and pay about it. However, at the very moment, I was writing the section about my interactions with the girls in the house, the message came through with the curriculum. It was so clear to me I was meant to be serving the house by teaching this class. I had been preaching for well over a year that we had to find a way for them to be attached to purpose when they graduated and began working. The message was loud and clear from God; I was meant to teach this class, and it didn't matter what else I had going on.

August 15th:

It was the second week of class. I wasn't exactly sure what the weekly curriculum would look like when I agreed to teach the class, but once we began, I was so glad I had said yes! It was definitely my jam! Each week we learned about how job training and skills align with God's call for your life. We learned about purpose and how you can walk in purpose in any line of (ethical and legal) career you choose. I was absolutely loving this class! It didn't hurt that I had a super eager student with an entrepreneurial spirit who could not wait to learn every lesson in the course! In the first week of class, I asked her what her expectations for the class were. She looked me straight in the eye and told me that she knew her passion, her purpose, and her career goals, but she had never done legal business before. She wanted to learn how to run a legal business. I shrugged my shoulders and grinned, telling her I thought that was a very reasonable expectation. That week we had started digging into job skills and how an unskilled laborer makes less per hour versus an employee with skills, education, and experience. I could see her eyes scan the pyramid on the page and land with defeat on the bottom level with the lowest pay. I acknowledged the skills versus income pyramid and then looked her dead in the eye and told her this pyramid did not define her. I told her when she exited the program and entered the workforce, she would inevitably be an unskilled laborer and start out with a lower wage. However, what she lacked in skills and experience, she could make up for with persistence, determination, work ethic, and grit. I explained how in our traditional business, a skilled laborer may come in making more per hour, but in the long run, an unskilled laborer can be trained in the way we want them to and work their way up to being more valuable with a higher pay scale.

I told her, "What you lack in skills, you make up for with work ethic." She got a sparkle in her eye, grinned ear to ear, and wrote down in her notes: "I am not defined by the pyramid." I then went on to ask her about her passions and dreams. She told me how much she loved skincare, makeup, and beauty; how she planned to get a job at Sephora or Ulta, attend cosmetology school, and eventually have her own skincare line. I asked her what the first obstacle she foresaw was. She looked at me pensively and asked, "Well, you're a business owner. Would you hire me as an employee if I was in the program?" I wanted to jump up and scream, "Yes! Yes! I would hire you! Right now! And, I would walk with you through the journey. I would mentor you in business and help you learn marketable skills. I would teach you purposeful business and what missional entrepreneurship looks like. I would help you see your value and attach you to a greater cause!"

But I didn't have a business that would allow me that freedom. None of my traditional business would be a fit, and my skincare business wasn't right either. It requires a great deal of networking, which is difficult to achieve when you've been in hiding for extended periods of time and can't associate with those that you do know. It's not impossible, but it is a challenging journey for someone in this situation. Instead, I smiled back across the table and told her, "Yes, I personally would hire you. I wouldn't care if you were in a program. I would be happy to see you were taking steps to turn your life around. But that's me, and I have a missional heart. Not all companies are like that, but more and more are starting up every day. We're not going to worry about that right now. We're going to pray about it and show up with our best foot first when the time comes." I walked into the director's office to sign the instructor log and sat down to chat with her about how the class was going. As we talked about the girls looking for jobs and their career paths, I decided to tell her about my vision. I explained that I wasn't sure if it was a one, five, or ten-year plan, but that it was definitely on my radar. She smiled back, pointed to the other room, and said, "Well, we certainly have employees ready for you."

I brought the subject up to my husband, and he said, "You are going to make money with this, right? You're not going to do this for free, are you?" I explained there would be a percentage of proceeds going to my partnerships, and we would have survivors on staff, but sure, I would make sure I didn't do it for free (entirely).

August 16th

I sent the kids off to school and sat down in my office to hammer some work out. The plan was to spend a large chunk of the day writing, so I could finish my book. However, when I sat down, I found myself googling "how to start a social enterprise" and "what to know when starting a hat company." I spent the entire day hashing out this plan. I wrote down the name and mission statement and even designed the logo. I mapped out who my target customer was, where they shopped, how much they spent on hats. I reached out to a local boutique and asked what the wholesale cost is of the hats she sells and what her markup is. I researched upcoming trends for fall 2020. I looked at the deadline for releasing a hat line for the upcoming fall. I researched my competition and analyzed their marketing approach. I created the business model and outlined my own personal marketing plan. I assessed start-up costs and how much operating cash I would need. I looked at production-related costs and realized I had a lot of questions. I studied steps to take to create an ethical, social enterprise that gets people excited about the mission. I worked on a pitch deck. I produced a finance plan. I named different styles of hats. I even looked into the biblical significance of a woman's head covering.

I read in Corinthians 11 about women covering their heads in prayer because man was created for Christ, but woman was the glory of man and created for man. It said, "That is why a wife ought to have a symbol of power on her head, because of the angels." I thought about this scripture. It could be hard for some to read, seeing that "woman was created for man." But, if you keep reading, you see that woman is the glory of man. These women don't know that lifestyle. They had been used for anything but glory. Biblical definition of glory: good reputation, honor, a result of being created in God's image. So, the woman's head covering was a reminder of the man's identity in Christ. With these hats, we could give the *power* back that was taken from these women. We could use the hats to restore their authority and remind men of their glory and what women were actually created for. And suddenly, it seemed like hats were the exact right choice for this social enterprise. I named my hats, writing down the names of every survivor I have had the privilege of knowing. I thought about each of their character and unique giftings. I thought about what type of hat would best represent each of them. I envisioned a photoshoot with each of these uniquely and marvelously made women wearing these hats. I thought of blog entries that would tell their stories of redemption. I imagined each of them working in this space, their hands touching the hats, and their minds creating alongside me. I thought about different skills they each had that could be built upon, honed, and strengthened.

I decided, in addition to the fashion hats, we would also have one universal, snap back with various words to choose from. I kept thinking that this hat would be called Rahab because we're all truly Rahab. In true transparency, I was thinking of Gomer to begin with. I searched Rahab on Bible Hub to read her story. I remembered immediately I had confused the two stories (There were apparently several harlots and prostitutes in the Bible God sanctified and used to tell stories of grace and redemption.) I read about Rahab, the former harlot called to heroism. I read about women like Rahab being sinned against more often than being the actual sinners but were left with the vile title. I thought about Rahab and her act of bravery. I thought about all the absolute crap my girls had been through in their life and how I tell them they are superheroes. I decided it was because of Rahab's lifestyle she was able to answer the call and not fear death by the king of Jericho for harboring the two spies. I thought about how a "pure" woman would have most likely been too afraid to accept the challenge. She saw the good in the men. She wasn't concerned about betraying her nation because she had most likely seen the worst of her nation. She was sanctified, not through her actions, but through the belief in her heart, once again exemplifying that even the worst of sinners can be saved from sin and hell through a heart connection. She birthed a lineage from which Jesus came. Rahab. That would be the name of our cap.

And then, I looked at everything I had written down and thought to myself, "That's great. But I have to finish this book first. After I've finished the book, I will continue exploring the idea of this hat company." I stared at my computer, trying to decide how to wrap this book up.

October 18th:

I looked back in my journal, where I had given myself a deadline for this book. October 18…. One year to the date from when I decided I would table the topic of the hat company until after I had finished my book… And I wept, with uncontrollable tears streaming down my face, as I sat in front of my computer.

I can't explain it unless you yourself have experienced such clear direction after an extended period of questioning God's call for your life. The crazy part is we can wonder in what feels like the wilderness for two and a half years. We can stand on an island in the midst of the storm, answering God's call, saying, "Yes, here I am Lord, send me. Your ways and not mine Lord. Where you lead, I'll follow. I will wait upon you and mount up with wings like eagles. Raise my hands, paint my spirit gold, bow my head, and keep my heart slow." You can sit in what feels like an eternity of being obedient and submissive without answers. And then suddenly, in an almost audible tone, you can hear your calling and direction spoken into your life. You can hear God's voice boldly proclaiming, "who knows but that you have come to your royal position for such a time as this."

It is this moment when you realize that the wilderness and the storms are part of your journey. It is in the wilderness where you are being forged and strengthened to fully step into your calling. It is what you do on that island in the midst of the storm that determines what your journey looks like. It is the growth and spiritual transformation that can occur in the middle of the wilderness that prepares us for the next chapter. But, you have to be willing to own your power and fulfill your purpose.

The Power Project

T he Power Project: A journey when one realizes their Purpose, Owns their God-given gifts, has the Wisdom to take action, is Empowered by God above, and Reaches those who need to hear the message God has given them. I started writing this book with a longing, a desire to create impact and bring about change. I was searching and yearning for the power to do so. What I had yet to realize was I didn't have to search for that power or even ask permission to embrace it. He, who is able to do far more abundantly than all that we ask or think, had instilled this power within me. It was branded upon my heart. I knew my gifts. I knew that I was being called to more. I just had to step into that call. I had to quit searching for permission or acceptance from outside sources. I had to quit questioning my gifts. I just simply needed to be obedient, listen, and follow Him on this journey. This journey of purpose. Don't just be inspired by my purpose journey. Answer the call and create your own.